Tribal Theory
The Genius of Anxiety, Depression & Trauma

"A deeply empowering perspective on healing that focuses on the innate wisdom of the body and soul."
Reilly Scott Singer/Songwriter

"Learning about Tribal Theory will bring us insight into why we behave the way we do and how we can use our unique gifts to our benefit. It will improve our relationships with our spouses, children, family members, work colleagues and most importantly, with ourselves. It is a priceless investment in ourselves and in our futures."
Darlene MacGillivray, Mother of three sons

"It was the idea of "should and should not" that got me excited about the book. Trauma is no body's favourite place to be. The language of moving forward and shifting the terms used to move through the trauma was known, but seeing it in writing and being able to go back to that again and again - because it is an interactive book, made it more real for me. It evoked positive feelings when reading it."
Weweshkiinzhigook Gooseeyes Girl
Rhonda Lee McIsaac MEd.,
Multidisciplinary Leadership,
Anishnaubek writer from Northernwestern Ontario

"It is exciting to see Tribal Theory flourish in our classroom tribe. In action, you witness young children celebrating the Homebody and Hunter strengths of each other while learning to work together to meet their authentic needs. Many behaviors, I once thought needed to be eliminated in the classroom are now celebrated for the gifts they truly bring to our tribe."
Carolyn McGuire OCT
Prime Minister's Award for Teaching Excellence 2016

I acknowledge that this book was written on the traditional, ancestral, and unceded territory of the Musqueam people.

Tribal Theory

The Genius of Anxiety, Depression

&

Trauma

Barbara Allyn

I would like to address the term "tribal" within Tribal Theory. The term tribe references all social groups including families, villages, nations, religions etc. While I understand the important use of the term with Indigenous communities, it is not meant to be, nor do I believe it to be in this context, culturally specific.

Editing by Michael Christopher

TribaLORE Arts + Science
www.tribaltheoryglobal.com

TRIBAL THEORY
THE GENIUS OF ANXIETY, DEPRESSION, & TRAUMA

Our bodies do not only simply remember. They prepare, serve, protect, and look for creative ways to integrate and make meaning of our experiences. This helps us to mitigate life's adversities and to prepare for and avoid future adversity and crisis. Anxiety correlates with our neurological and nervous system response; depression is the recognition of the oppression of the authentic self and trauma pays acute attention to the infliction of moral injury.

Our bodies exist to serve and protect us through their own forms of intelligence. We innately embody protective responses and survival techniques in order to live. Responses formed and refined since the beginning of life itself. Anxiety, depression and trauma are not mental disorders, mental deficiencies, or mental illness. They are clues, warnings, calls to action in response to being dis-placed from our authentic selves. A dis-order, a disruption of the nurturing of our own nature both spiritually and physically. They are a recognition of this imbalance, a presentation of survival tactics in response to something that has happened to us, not that something is wrong with us. They are *the markings of the Genius* that is the human body responding to adversity, asking us to examine and integrate our experiences. To journey to where we have a sense of self, safety and belonging.

Anxiety is a natural fear response to keep us and others safe. Depression is a sign of the oppression of our minds, bodies and spirit when we have ignored our authentic self and purpose. Trauma serves to dissociate us from meaningless tragedy, creating timeless travel in an effort to stay alive when our pillars of moral and core beliefs (spiritual, cultural, physical and philosophical) have been denounced, disturbed, or destroyed. Other so-called mental disorders, like ADHD or ADD, are really only abilities that no longer fit in with our modern western environment but have always been and continue to be essential if we are to survive and thrive. To label these as mental disorders is inaccurate. This is the genius of the human body that evolved in our ancestry and which without we would likely not exist at all. Misunderstood, undermined, and even demonized in our current Western mental health framework, this genius needs to be once again revealed, witnessed, and respected.

Tribal Theory acknowledges this Genius and responds with a healing framework that witnesses the body's story and responds by nurturing the individual nature in all of us.

NOTE: I hope readers will also familiarize themselves with writings about the Gut Brain and the Vagus Nerve, essential material that can be woven within the Tribal Theory framework.

TO

Connie, Marilyn, Winnifred,
Wade, Rose & Stacey

You are earth angels with your wings tucked in.

CONTENTS

The Origin
About This Book

Other Applications
Author's Note

ACKNOWLEDGMENTS

To my loving family and friends who have always given me a safe place to land.

To the global communities who have welcomed me, taken my hand and opened my heart and soul to their world of healing. I am forever grateful.

To the animals in all of our lives, who care for us unconditionally and greet us like we are great.

"Sometimes the questions are complicated and the answers are simple." Dr. Seuss

THE ORIGIN

I stood at the door of my office and looked down the hall to the waiting room. Another hour was coming to an end, and the doors of several other offices opened as our adolescent clients completed their counselling sessions. I often experienced sadness at this hourly ritual. The body language and facial expressions of our young clients often left me with the impression that they understood themselves as misfits; as people who did not belong.

This day, however, as my next young client walked toward me, adorned in tattoos and piercings, the scars of self-harm marking her collar bones, I observed something different. What I saw was a 'tribal' person. Her body told a different story, a new story. It elucidated who she now had become; a proclamation of her right to exist, marking her place in her Tribe.

In that flash of recognition, it became clear to me tha
those behaviours and symptoms which my colleagues an
I routinely interpreted and treated as disorders
dysfunctions, and diseases were, in fact, natural and ofte
creative expressions of deeper and more fundamenta
needs which were not being met; the need to understanc
and subsequently live from our authentic place in ou
Tribe.

My 'tribal' youth entered my office. I shut the door, took a
marker to my whiteboard, and drew three circles within
one other. In the outer circle I wrote 'Hunter', in the
middle circle 'Guard', and in the inner circle, 'Homebody'
At the top of the board I wrote and underlined 'Your Tribe'
In the session that unfolded, this simple drawing of three
circles came alive with meaning for both of us. Together
my young client and I explored where she felt she woulc
belong if she were to belong to a Tribe. Our discoverie:
that session would prove to be transformative.

In the succeeding decades, I have employed these
three circles and this tribal approach, since named **Tribal
Theory**, as I have worked in crisis response and trauma, as
well as clinical and family work. Tribal Theory has proven
indispensable in frontline crisis work, mediation,
workshops, training and counselling. It has been used
effectively by social workers, first responders, medical and
military workers, parents, teachers, and families, and in

innumerable coffee shop chats with everyone who has shown interest.

What has emerged has been a nearly universally accepted framework, one that has allowed for better understanding of ourselves and others. By 're-visioning' our place in our tribe through a broader and deeper explanation of how our responses to trauma have affected us personally and globally, our relationships have been renewed and revitalized. Tribal Theory allows us to accept our place in our Tribe and to begin to value our unique being.

Tribal Theory does not emphasize 'being disordered', but examines the source of our pain - which, in this framework, is 'being displaced'. When displaced we present ourselves with maladaptive behaviours and dysfunctions both in mind and in body. Behaviours are clues. To understand each personal story of displacement is to find a map toward personal healing. To find personal healing is to make meaning of one's story. It is the genesis of new meaning - the discovery of the genius of anxiety, depression, and trauma - that is the key to witnessing and making meaning of our experiences, healing, and evolving.

"We shall not cease from exploration. And at the end of all our exploring will be to arrive where we started and know the place for the first time."   T.S. Eliot

ABOUT THIS BOOK

You are part of your Tribe. Your story plays an important role in understanding Tribal Theory. This book is designed to be interactive so that you can reflect and consider while you read. In the writing of this book, I have tried to communicate the concepts of Tribal Theory in the same everyday language and structure from which it has evolved.

'Tribal Theory, The Genius of Anxiety, Depression & Trauma' is a place for you to discover, and even play with the story of who you are. There are blank journal pages throughout the book for your own notes, ideas, and thoughts, and even the personal stories of others that may inspire you in re-telling your own.

You will be introduced to the Tribal Theory framework as well as the integrative practices of Sensory Dialogue, Symbolics, the Trauma Life Line, and you will discover how trauma is a presentation of Moral Injury.

This book includes Illustrations & Considerations, 'in the moment' counselling examples, and TribaLORE - interviews showcasing the stories of those who have used the theory.

There are also pages marked 'Walkabout'. These are the breadcrumbs of ideas that have evolved alongside Tribal Theory and they are designed to enhance its meaning.

You are encouraged to bring everything within you to the table while you interact with this book and learn more about Tribal Theory. Explore your authentic role in your Tribe and reconstruct your story in order to celebrate who you are. Learn about how others in the Tribe respond and use this new awareness as a guide to help you to understand the actions taken by those around you.

Immersion into Tribal Theory is often rapid. Tribal Theory helps one identify their authentic selves and their place in their social Tribe. When one discovers one's genius - one's place - they discover new wisdom, freedom, and creativity. While making meaning of your life story by discovering the missing puzzle pieces, your gifts of protection and survival are put in place. A new picture emerges and a new understanding begins.

Tribal Theory is the framework but the story is written by you.

TRIBAL THEORY

TRIBAL THEORY

'Home is not where you were born, home is where your attempts to escape cease.' - Naguib Mahfouz

THE TRIBE

We are all born into the Human Social Tribe.
As a Member of the Tribe, to thrive, each of us needs to be celebrated for our natural gifts and abilities and encouraged to assume the role that fits with our truest, most authentic self.
Although roles in the Tribe differ, each person also needs to be recognized and valued.

When one is able to live in and from their authentic role in the Tribe, they feel a sense of ease, order, and place.
They belong.

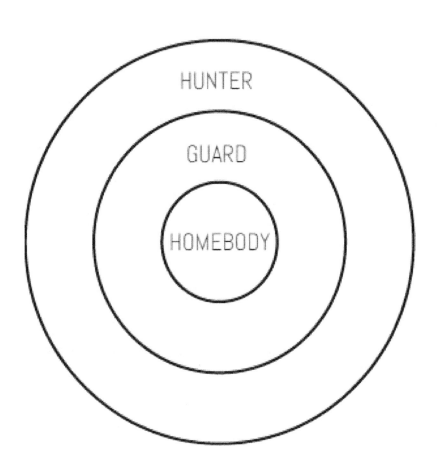

THE TRIBAL CIRCLES

The three circles represent the primal roles in a Tribe.

With each of these roles come characteristics and ways of being that contribute to the survival of the Tribe. Each of us has our primal place in the Tribe, a place where we best fit. When we are rooted in our primal place in the Tribe, we flourish.

The transformative power of Tribal Theory first reveals itself when you begin to identify your authentic role.

The two foundational roles in the Tribe are the Hunter, represented by the outer circle, and the Homebody, drawn as the inner circle. The middle circle is the Guard. The Guard is a circumstantially 'evoked' organic radar detection and response component, a part of both the Hunter and the Homebody, that is accessed or 'called into being' when a real or perceived threat from an environment occurs and a protector is required. The Guard component will be explored in further depth later in the book.

Let's look at the respective roles of the Hunter and the Homebody.

HOW DO I KNOW IF I AM A HUNTER OR A HOMEBODY?

The discovery of one's authentic role can be instantaneous for some and require more exploration for others. As you read, consider the activities you loved as a child. Perhaps you enjoyed exploring the outdoors and wildlife, making colourful crafts, riding your bike down steep hills, or making intricate indoor reading forts out of blankets.

Try to remember where you most distinctly felt that you were being you, where your sense of wonder and curiosity seemed most alive, where you felt a sense of safety and a full sense of presence.

For those who have blurred memories of childhood, this may be more of an exploration. Just see what resonates naturally.

THE AUTHENTIC HUNTER

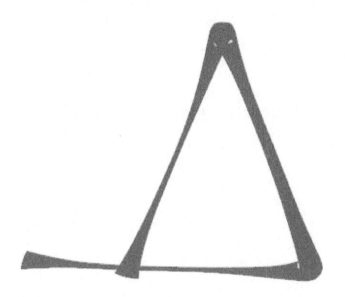

A D H D

Attention Directed in a Higher Dimension

THE AUTHENTIC HUNTER

NATURE & SPIRIT

"not all those that wander are lost"

J.R.R. Tolkien

A Hunter's Tale

I don't know why, but I couldn't stand sitting at my desk in middle school. I would rush, on the first day of school, to grab a seat by the window. In fact, I would worry for nights in anticipation of that first day, anxiously preparing how I was going to beat my classmates to a window desk. I would do practice runs from my front door to the school, timing myself, while guessing which class I would be in and how long it would take to get there. I would open my window at night and consciously try to send my feelings of being trapped in school again out the window while taking big whiffs of the fall leaves outside. That smell made me feel better. To this day, I purposely scope out places that feel open, whether it be a bus seat, office desk or place in a crowd and I still run a lot, in the woods by a creek.

First year university student diagnosed with ADHD

The Hunter embraces instinctive tracking, hunting, and survival skills in order to meet the essential nourishment of the Tribe. Naturally gifted with ADHD – Attention Directed in a Higher Dimension - a Hunter is restless, always moving, and resting only long enough to move again. Hunters are born with an innate, spiritual understanding of, and connection with, nature. Hunters respond in movement. Hunters provide the energy needed to survive. Hunters are story-makers.

Most of us have experienced a person who won't sit still. The student in the classroom is a great example. One of the telling characteristics of a Hunter is that, without being able to 'move towards something' and literally use 'hunting' strategies in daily life, school, work, and play, these individuals experience a sense of being trapped. Their need to be moving, resting only in order to be able to move again, conflicts with the conventions of most classrooms and workplaces, as well as the expectations of many other environments. The ways that hospitals, shelters, detention centres, and courts of law are built represent confinement. All of these create a sense of being caged to a Hunter.

A Hunter embodies ADHD, or what Tribal Theory refers to as 'Attention Directed in a Higher Dimension'. The symptoms of ADHD, as diagnosed in the world of westernized mental health, are the gifts which a tribal Hunter would require to survive in the wild.

16

The Hunter is continuously strategizing and tends to interrupt in conversation. This may create the impression that they are not paying attention, or not listening, but this is often far from the truth. Hunters are almost always paying attention acutely, but only to what they find interesting or pertinent. While listening, they are preparing to do what they may need to do in order to Hunt, or to prevent becoming the hunted themselves.

Hunters are hyper aware of their surroundings and quickly intuit the people around them. These are both abilities that are required to carry out their authentic role.

This awareness and intuition, this ability to see patterns in communication is uncanny and all too often, hunters know what is going to be said next and jump in in order to 'move' the conversation forward. This alertness and seemingly obstructive attempt to 'get to the point' is the product of decision making abilities and the need to problem solve while in flight or movement. It is acting on impulse, as is often required in flight.

For Hunters, thinking the 'worst first' is an inherent way of being. They see worst case scenarios and strategize to prevent them. Hunters like to solve problems. They are able to move away from the worst outcome and take measures to prevent the worst from happening. Often extroverted in nature, their intuition allows them to predict and prevent problems. However, if there is no problem to solve, the Hunter will usually create a

17

challenge in order to keep themselves busy and hone these inherent skills.

Hunters need to be connected, holistically, to nature to feed their authentic way of being. The wild one is one with nature, where there are no straight lines, and where unknown danger waits around every bend. The adventurous spirit of the Hunter, in their authentic role, has them 'run to' nature, creating stories and taking risks that build and integrate coping strategies and cultivate a sense of worth.

WALKABOUT

Flight/energy surge is the response of a Hunter. They have a built in biological gift which enables them to respond quickly when needed. The ability to call on adrenalin is an extremely helpful survival response whether to save oneself or protect the tribe. To run towards the Hunt or to run away from danger.

TribaLORE: Douglas

Douglas grew up in Ottawa with two younger sisters, and parents who functioned from opposite ends of the emotional spectrum. His mother is an unconditionally loving and supportive parent. His father, who himself grew up with military discipline, was an angry figure who's fluctuating moods controlled the household.

Douglas's relationship with his father, from whom he inherited similar anger issues, remained complicated until his father's death a decade ago. He was left with complex and difficult feelings, and turned to drugs, alcohol, and a dangerous lifestyle as coping mechanisms instead of responsibly dealing with and processing his grief.

"My lifestyle led me to a lot of terrible things. I gravitated towards unhealthy male role models instead of good, healthy people. I sought out dangerous people who had my back no matter what happened; I developed a sort of evil support system. I was pretending to be something that I wasn't."

Working in the fine dining industry, parties ceased to be parties. Life was spinning out of control. During this time, Douglas also developed unhealthy relationship patterns. He chronically got involved with toxic partners, and the situations always ended badly. His final relationship and subsequent breakup ended with a suicide attempt.

"I was falling in love with any girl who would have me, and then I would let it destroy me. Everything was falling apart. It was a tornado of garbage. It wasn't just the booze and the drugs - it was also the anger."

After one completely out of control night, Douglas realized that he had a choice: either get sober, or likely die as the result of his lifestyle. He couldn't understand how things had progressed to this point. His mother, ever supportive, had introduced him to Barbara Allyn and Tribal Theory some months earlier. He called her and told her that he knew if he had another night like that, he would die. He was instructed to make a move.

Douglas made a promise to himself to become well - and on his own terms. He detoxed from drugs and alcohol, and developed methods that worked for him. He cut out most of the people he knew. He compartmentalized what was going wrong in his life, and approached each issue separately. He allowed any criticism of his approaches to fuel his motivation. Life began to take off for him right away. Leang into his experience as a graffiti artist, he organized an art show to showcase his work, and it was a wild success. Then, suddenly, the COVID-19 pandemic erupted, and he knew that his art practice would no longer be a sustainable source of income. Instead of becoming frustrated, because of the work he had been doing in Tribal Theory, Douglas saw this as an opportunity to continue to thrive.

"I'm restless, I'm a Hunter, I need to stay occupied. Because of Tribal Theory, I knew who I am and I was armed with the framework and the tools to continue to succeed in life."

Douglas developed his interest in off-grid living and gardening into a fully-functioning urban produce farm in his backyard. He brought in a number of friends to help and now supplies to restaurants in his region. He has spent his summer farming, hiking, and camping. He has intentionally avoided relationships since becoming sober.

"It would be so easy to check out for a night and not deal with everything that's going on, but I will get through it with a sober, clear mind. The amount of energy I used to put into partying, I now put towards this purpose. I can't believe this is my life right now."

"Tribal Theory opened up a whole new chapter of my life. I'm not a caged animal anymore. I'm a roaming Hunter chasing my purpose. How can I deny myself of that?

NOTES

NOTES

THE AUTHENTIC HOMEBODY

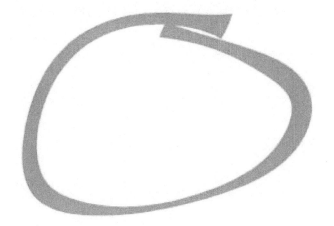

A D D

Attention to Double Detail

THE AUTHENTIC HOMEBODY
NURTURE & HEART

"the ache for home lives in all of us, the safe place where we can go as we are and not be questioned" Maya Angelou
A Homebody's Tale

When people say "go to your Happy Place", I immediately think of the blanket forts that I built as a kid. My mom would help me drape huge blankets over the dining room table, and I would keep the chairs tucked in underneath the table, using them as little shelves for the collection of tiny plastic figurines that I got from fast food restaurants. I would gather my stuffed animals and have tea parties or read books out loud, believing that no one, except my stuffed friends, could hear me. I would sing a song about wiggling and I remember laughing to myself so hard that my stomach hurt the next day. That feeling didn't really hurt though; it reminded me of my laughter and it made me smile. A firefighter's reflection when asked about a childhood safe place.

The Homebody is the nesting heart of the Tribe. The most distinct characteristic of the Homebody is their delight in others, and their comfort in being themselves. They are the nurturers of the heart. They love to love, love to be loved, and do not find purpose in competing with others. They care for others, but, because they like themselves as well, enjoy spending time alone. That time alone is dedicated to discovery; to research, play and create, and to pay attention to details. Homebodies possess the gift of observing details, and, in doing so, acquire the knowledge required to meet the needs of others. The Homebody learns to create an environment for both Hunters and other Homebodies to come to; a safe place to be authentic.

Unlike Hunters, Homebodies do not need to be in constant movement and often prefer to sit in contemplative thought, or to curl up with a book. Homebodies, like hunters, are also intuitive, but their intuition is different. Whereas the Hunter is intuitive with 'problem solving', the Homebody is intuitive in 'reading others', and assessing who is friend or foe. This is a protective quality which keeps those who might harm or threaten others away from the safe place. Homebodies are not about problem solving as much as stopping a problem before it starts. Homebodies are not concerned with crisis management or damage control, but with preventative measures which reduce hypothetical threat; turning

28

unknown danger into manageable risk.

Homebodies do best in a closed environment with other Homebodies and are perfectly capable of communicating with others if brought into a conversation. They are great listeners as this is their way of ascertaining who is and who is not safe. Identifying from the heart, the Homebody can easily give their own heart away if they feel a kinship or trust with someone. If they are corrected or criticized, they exploit the opportunity to grow.

Homebodies require time alone. Unlike the Hunter, who thrives in movement, the Homebody needs to be still and alone to process information, make sense of it, and act upon it. Hunters run; Homebodies research.

The Homebody's nesting instincts are strong and Tribal Theory suggests that, although they always had a role in the Tribe in nomadic times, their role of nurturer developed further as humans began to settle in one place for longer periods of time and, in turn, now represent the hearth, the heart, and the home.

No longer required to be continuously on the move, stable homes became safe places to live, learn, and to land. Thus, the Homebody's place in the Tribe was encouraged to evolve. Homebodies began to hold community together. Often the quiet participators, they listen and engage as they create a sense of safety and wellbeing. Homebodies create a caring, holistic space for others, preparing the nourishment required for the mind, body & spirit and preserving Tribal wisdom through storytelling.

NOTES

WALKABOUT

Freeze/focus is the response of a Homebody. They have a built in biological gift which enables them to sustain focus. This ability is an extremely helpful survival response as it helps to heighten and engage the body's sensory functions. To 'pick up or sense' dangerous beings who enter one's safe space.

TribaLORE: Grace

Grace, at fourteen years of age, now identifies as an empathic Homebody who is grateful for parents who have always inspired and supported her in her compassion and desire to help others.

"My parents are very giving people and I always aspire to be like them. When I was in grade four, I made a pact with myself to make sure that I wasn't ever leaving any other kids out."

Grace is very attuned to the energy and stories of others and was experiencing a lot of anxiety in social situations, particularly while attending school. This anxiety had manifested in some maladaptive behaviours. Grace had spent most of her life feeling that she hadn't any control over her emotions. She would often feel overwhelmed. As she grew older, her self-image and self worth worsened and, along with it, her health. She threw herself into an extremely intense workout routine to distance from painful feelings. In doing so, Grace felt that she was protecting herself from experiencing negative feelings.

"It felt really great at the time. Things bothered me less and I didn't really hang out with anyone anymore, even my family. It felt like such a relief."

Grace's parents observed this change in her and knew they had to do something. They took her to the hospital where her heart rate was found to be so low that she was admitted. This was a turning point for Grace, and where she was first introduced to Tribal Theory. She began to understand that she is a homebody and rediscovered her natural gifts. She is an intuitive empath. She began exploring her own trauma. Gaining this new understanding of herself, Grace began to see connections between many of her personal challenges and her way of being in the world. Tribal Theory provided her with a new perspective, a creative lens to see how she walks in the world, a new way to see her authentic gifts.

"A discovery I've made is how I felt my whole life that I was stupid and that I was the lowest student. But I was never the lowest student; I was just sensing and picking up emotions of people who felt like they were the lowest students. I figured out that I was a Homebody and that they tend to not nurture themselves and that just really gave me a lot of relief. I was just looking at an evil disease that was living inside of me and it didn't feel right cause I still felt like me."

As Grace continues her journey she reflectively shares her hopes for others struggling with similar stories.

"The public system will call it a mental illness and tell you that there's something wrong with you or your brain, but it's really nothing to do with that. Everything you're going through is connected to the trauma that's happened in your life, to not being or knowing your authentic self. It is important to understand so you can heal your background and find out for yourself, where you belong."

"This is your story. This is not anyone else's."

NOTES

WALKABOUT

People who live on the street are often referred to as Homeless but not all need a roof over their heads to survive. Some need to keep moving to meet the needs of their authentic selves.

Hunters are Hard to House.

Homebodies are Homeless.

NOTES

THE GUARD

THE GENIUS PROTECTOR

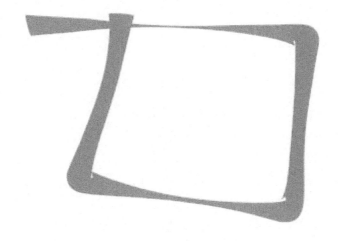

THE HEALTHY GUARD
The Genius
as the
WISE GUIDE

"You have the gift of a brilliant internal guardian that stands ready to warn you of hazards and guide you through risky situations."

Gavin de Becker

The amygdalae are two small almond shaped structures (the name comes from the Greek word 'almond') located near the hippocampus in the frontal portion of the temporal lobe in the brain. They initiate the body's response to threat and seem to modulate many of our reactions to events that are important to survival.

In Tribal Theory the response to threat is governed by the Guard. Both the Hunter and the Homebody invoke the Guard when threatened. The Guard is what Gavin de Becker calls "the gift of fear". It possesses a sensory-like intuition, with an ability to see warning signs and subsequently to prepare survival strategies quickly. It is the holistic genius responding to threatening situations with appropriate adrenalin releases that manifest as flight, fight, or freeze responses. As the Healthy Guard responds and solves problems in situations, it builds a foundation which then integrates and makes meaning of what has happened. This 'guidance' can then be called upon when other challenges arise.

When a person is living in their authentic role (Homebody or Hunter) they will summon what Tribal Theory recognizes as their Healthy Guard in order to deal with momentary adversity and crisis. The Healthy Guard does its job then steps back until its service is next required. It is a daily survival tool, a gift of protection, a primal fear that can only be extinguished with direct consequence. It is our early responder; the first gift of fear on the scene.

THE FEAR GUARD

The Genius
as the

HYPERVIGILANT PROTECTOR

"You fear that if you lower your guard for even one second your whole world will disintegrate into chaos."

Douglas Coupland

So, what happens if someone is pushed or forced out of their authentic role due to adversity, crisis or trauma? (If a Hunter is forced to take up a Homebody role or vice versa.)

Tribal Theory calls this being DISPLACED.

In forced displacement, under threat, the Healthy Guard is replaced by what Tribal Theory calls the Fear Guard. This is when the Genius responds with its hyper vigilant protector. Forced out of their Authentic role and place, where a sense of belonging exists, the Fear Guard usurps the Healthy Guard. The Fear Guard is unable to make meaning of the threatening circumstances and moves beyond simply trying to protect, to fearfully trying to control the environment in order to keep the tribe safe. In this attempt to control everything, the Fear Guard becomes hyper vigilant, making it difficult to process and make meaning of circumstances. If one cannot make meaning of circumstances, one cannot move out of the Fear Guard, even once a threat diminishes or ends. Displaced, a sense of dis-order is established. One will try to control their environment by attempting to recreate order. When one is displaced from one's authentic self, one cannot recreate or maintain order. This struggle leaves the displaced with the feeling that there is something wrong with them, that they are broken; a misfit.

Unable, in fear guard, to make meaning, protective and creative protection gifts that worked as an authentic Hunter or Homebody turn into maladaptive responses while displaced. Maladaptive behaviours can present themselves as anxiety, depression, panic attacks, sleep disturbances, ritualized behaviour, self-medicating, self-harm, social disconnection, dissociation, and thoughts of worthlessness. Recognized as disorders in the mental health field, in Tribal Theory, these are symptoms of displacement. The Genius is trying to tell us that we are out of order, ease, and place.

In a hypervigilant Fear Guard state, unable to integrate experiences, we cannot tap into the Healthy Guard that makes meaning of and actually helps us solve challenges. The Fear Guard remains at the frontline, prepared for something else bad to happen at any moment. This attentive Fear Guard, which presents as anxiety, depression and trauma, is our First Responder. It will stand guard until we are in the safe place where we belong.

Note: A person can choose to step into a role that is not their natural, authentic role, and function well in what would otherwise be a 'displaced' position if they preserve their authentic selves while doing so.

THE YOUNG HUNTER
ILLUSTRATION & CONSIDERATION

You began living with your maternal grandmother after your mother died in a ski accident. You were nine years old when the accident happened and, although your father was not with your mother at the time of the accident, your maternal grandmother was always referring to how your father failed to protect your mother. In your eyes, this insinuated that it was your father's fault. You and your mother were authentic Hunters; your father, a Homebody. You always recognized and understood the tragic loss that this was to your father and how your grandmother's insinuation, that he could not keep his partner safe, was devastating to him while you watched him slip further and further into a depression, while your grandmother assumed the role of Homebody. Even at the age of nine you knew that you needed to protect him from your grandmother's blame and shame and you started to stay home more and focus on your father. Spending time with him, trying to be encouraging, doing your best to keep his depression at bay. In doing so, you are displaced. You pull away from your own activities, Hunter games, friends, and adventures to try and control your father's environment to protect him and guard him. This imposed role creates anxiety as you now spend more time thinking about what could happen to your father if you were not there to watch over him. The changing of the Healthy Guard to Fear Guard takes hold.

TribaLORE: Wilhelmina

Wilhelmina was born in Kitchener. Her parents split up when she was three, and divorced just after she turned five. As a child, she didn't speak; her older sister did all the speaking for her. Wilhelmina began speech and play therapy very young, attending counselling up to three times a week until she was eighteen. Her mother moved to Toronto and while Wilhelmina attended up to seventeen different schools, she began to experience behavioural issues. Wilhelmina's mom worked two jobs, and she and her sister mostly fended for themselves.

"Looking back on it, I'm like, wow, I really admire my mom for doing that. Cause that's a tough thing to do. She always tried to move us to a good area, better than the last one. We always tried to get better and she also did stuff for me, like the counseling, just so I had somebody to talk to, which I understand now; as a kid I hated the counseling. Then I became a teenager and the rebellion really started."

Her father remarried and had three more children with his new spouse, who had no interest in behaving as a parent to his daughters. Wilhelmina and her sister went from seeing her father once every other weekend to once a year.

"When I became a teenager, I was fed up with the fighting. I was fed up with the counseling. I was fed up with, you know, my mom not being there and fed up cause my dad's not there. I ran away from home."

As she transitioned to street life, Wilhelmina began using drugs. She felt like she had it under control at first, but she hated the feeling of being sober.

"I was always trying to fit into this box because I thought no one's gonna like the true and real me; I came with all this baggage. They would know that I go to counseling so they'd probably think I was messed up in the head. They would know that my parents split up and that my dad's a chicken, but, really, I have this great big family who totally loves me and supports me. And then they would say, well, you're a farce. You're not like the rest of us who have been abused by our fathers and stepfathers. I was always afraid of actually being myself."

Living on the streets Wilhelmina still felt afraid to be her authentic self and lived in fear.

"I was more afraid to be exactly who I was because I had more friends when I was high and felt that no one was going to like me for the actual little girl that I am. People liked me because I had drugs and because I can get high with them and somehow always have things under control. They felt safe with me, but then when I was sober I was scared of the world. I was scared of absolutely everything."

Eventually, Wilhelmina experienced trauma when, in a case of mistaken identity, she was kidnapped and nearly killed. Returning to her mother's house, Wilhelmina saw this as an opportunity to get off drugs.

"Like that song; you gotta know when to hold them, and you've got to know when to fold them. This was my chance to fold it. I had to be done with this."

Tribal theory helped Wilhelmina transition back into safe and sustainable home living. Through this work, Wilhelmina learned that she was a Hunter and that, throughout her life, she had been most unhappy when she was forced into a Homebody role. Wilhelmina began to reveal her authentic self.

"If you actually have to stay there for a long time, it takes a real toll on you. You find yourself disconnected because it's not where you should be. You're not doing the stuff that you should be doing."

Once Wilhelmina had a grasp on Tribal Theory, she began applying it to her life. Her husband has read this book, as well. They have used it together to identify their core individual aspects that need attention, and to remain their authentic selves, both separately and as a couple. In her workplace, Tribal theory has allowed Wilhelmina to identify her colleague's strengths and to then delegate and communicate to those strengths. She uses it to understand the many tribes she belongs to in her professional and personal life, and encourages others to understand and use the theory as well.

"It's a new skill. It's learning about yourself, learning about the people who are close to you."

"Be your authentic self because that is way more beautiful and attractive than someone who is trying to hide it all the time."

WALKABOUT

Displaced Hunters explode

Displaced Homebodies implode

DISPLACEMENT

THE DISPLACED HUNTER

Trying to force a Hunter to stay still for an extended period will not go well; they will feel confined and trapped.

The natural adrenaline response of a trapped Hunter is flight. Physically, they intuitively know how to respond. When pushed into Fear Guard, a Hunter feels backed into a corner. This heightens their flight response which is often misunderstood. It presents as oppositional, non-compliant, and defiant. Within institutional environments, the Hunter is often referred to as a 'flight risk".

The gift of the Hunter is their constant awareness, or Attention Directed in a Higher Dimension (ADHD). In Fear Guard, this presents a psychological and physiological challenge. It is observed as an attention deficit, and hyper dis-order. The Hunter's spiritual nature, however, captured in Fear Guard, will cause the Hunter to feel as though they are now prey.

In Fear Guard, Hunters present with helplessness, depression, sleep deprivation, consistent heightened awareness, and obsessive and compulsive patterns, which includes repetitive talking.

Disconnecting, unwillingly, from nature for any period of time, the Hunter becomes spiritually and physically dis-eased. They will suffer the same ailments, mentally and physically, as that of a caged animal.

When pushed into Fear Guard, Hunters present with helplessness and depression; they cannot perform their duty of helping to nourish others. They experience sleep deprivation as their heightened awareness keeps them alert at all times.

Panic attacks present themselves, accompanied by the feeling of being in a movie, of being watched or watching from the outside, and by tunnel vision. The panic feeling will be marked as a need to run away; to run to.

Physical ailments show up in the lower colon, muscles and nerves. Trapped in Fear Guard, the Hunter presents with dis-eases that are 'hard to pin down' like fibromyalgia and chronic fatigue.

When a displaced Hunter cannot move, they respond in ways that appear maladaptive but which are actually the genius strategies springing from attempts to escape from a sense of entrapment, and to carry out their authentic role in the Tribe.

They will find ways to leave their bodies, by wandering, running away in their minds, and dissociating. The Hunter is meeting the need to move, to run 'toward' the Hunt, and to connect spiritually with nature. Connection and interaction with nature is their only way to survive.

NOTES

THE DISPLACED HUNTER STORY

I loved to play outdoors when I was little. I loved the smell of dirt, wet leaves, and finding that 'perfect' stick. I would come in with my treasures from the backyard and pile them near the back door like a tower of discoveries. I would even sneak out of my bed at night to visit these treasures and go back to bed wondering what I may find tomorrow.

It was dark. I remember that because, when I heard the screaming, I awoke from my sleep and couldn't see anything. It was a terrible scream and it took me seconds to realize that it was my mother. I remember seeing my body moving in front of me, like I was watching myself, as I ran down the stairs. I ran into the kitchen and standing by the back door was a strange man holding my mother, his hand over her mouth, her eyes bulging. He looked me right in the eye, let go of my mother, and ran out the door. My mom fell to the floor and I rushed to her side. She told me to call 911 and I rushed to our wall phone, it was a bright bird's egg blue, and phoned for help. It was the first time that I heard the words 'home invasion'. I remember thinking it made our home sound like a scary place. The police told me how brave I had been, especially at my age, which was seven. I didn't feel brave. I felt changed. I felt that the inside was no longer safe from the outside and that the outside was scary. Like someone was in the bushes or in the trees, watching me. The next day I put on a pair of garden gloves, as to not touch the former treasures which now held the evil of the outside and threw them into a neighbour's leaf pile for them to deal with. I never used the back door again, though I would check it several times every night, three times actually, to make sure it was locked. I stopped playing outside. I hated being inside but felt unsafe outside. I had a duty now, to be close and protect my mom. Then the night terrors started.

43 year old with former addiction to cocaine and a current sleep disorder

TribaLORE: Jordan

Growing up in a typical family of five, Jordan and his two older brothers followed in the technical footsteps of their dad, who worked in mining. The three boys achieved even greater success as a result of furthering their education, throughout thier journeys, but to Jordon something did not *feel* right.

"It was very technical work involving objects and materials," explains Jordan. "I remember not really enjoying the work and only working to get through it. I was a sensitive child and my mom added that I was always empathic and eager to listen to other people's stories."

At the young age of 21 with a bachelors degree in electrical engineering, Jordan accepted his first job far away from home. "My dad encouraged me to take the opportunity," says Jordan. "But I was living in a place where I was not connected to the things that I enjoyed, like nature and family."

This disconnect manifested into physical symptoms. Jordan was eating poorly, and had such high stress that he developed a severe diagnosis of ulcerative colitis. Uncertain about the root causes of his deteriorating health, Jordan decided to move closer to home in hopes that the change in environment would help to solve his health problems.

"I felt better for a while, but I started to experience more mental health-related symptoms. At one point I even thought I had a brain tumour. I couldn't remember things and had major issues falling asleep. I also picked up smoking, which was against my healthy athletic nature. I remember thinking if I stay here doing this for the next 20 years I will deeply regret it and I felt a lack of value in my contributions. My own suffering led me to explore how I could support others. It made me feel proud and I connected to not only the work but myself as well.

Finally, Jordan made the decision to step away from his family's expectations and follow his own path towards counselling psychology.

"It was a difficult transition. I had my mom's support, but my brothers did not see or understand my depression and my dad was a bit let down because I was not following in his footsteps anymore. I felt I had to prove to my family that I really wanted to change. Their negative responses spurred me on to live my life for myself because for a long time I was living my life according to how I was seen by others."

Jordan's health improved, and as he explored this new

career path, a new awareness about his family started to emerge. Looking back, he recognized the shortcomings in how his family communicated; often with a lot of yelling and judging towards one another for possessing various moral flaws. Jordan also began to see that what our culture normally stigmatizes or perceives as a weakness can actually be seen as a gift. He began to see his ADHD diagnosis as a strength that empowered him to persist in life, and to engage with new activities and ways of thinking. He began viewing his family heritage through a new lens and connecting deeper with his roots and heritage.

"In 2016 I went to Italy, and it was a mind-blowing experience to meet all my Italian family for the first time. I met all these relatives who lived with my "symptoms"; talking with your hands, talking loudly, often yelling, and highly expressive with emotion. I understood that this was culturally their norm. In Canada, my family might be seen as being aggressive or even rude. However, in the right context these "abnormalities" may not be so abnormal after all!

THE DISPLACED HOMEBODY

When displaced, Homebodies move inward and blame themselves for failing to keep others safe. They feel responsible to represent home at all times.

In efforts to create a family, they work hard to rescue others. Their need to create a safe place is also, in part, a need to belong. In Fear Guard, this desperate effort to engage with others and connect can lead to risky behaviours.

The desire for family-like social connection, for reciprocated intimate connection, can lead to indulgence in alcohol and drugs that enhance social connection, and to exploitive, abusive relationships. A Homebody's response to fear is to freeze physically and emotionally. Because the Homebody processes internally, this dilemma causes a type of generalized anxiety - a 'what if' panic response - as well as feelings of hopelessness and worthlessness.

A Homebody presents with ADD, or Attention to Double Detail. In their Healthy Guard, a Homebody's role is to pay great attention to who is entering the safe place. When pushed into Fear Guard, ADD is heightened and presents as maladaptive.

A Homebody's natural urge to collect and stock up for emergencies and invest in the material things which they believe to possess symbolism may turn into hoarding. Negative self-talk spirals into feelings of hopelessness. Perfectionism is present. Body image issues emerge. In fear guard, OCD, referred to by Tribal Theory as Only Caring and Daring (and Daring to Care) presents as perseverating thought.

The Homebody's natural gift to intuit and provide for others needs turns inward, into a fear of failing to provide.

The Homebody is often capable of conveying an appearance of outward confidence but mercilessly questions themselves internally. Homebodies in Fear Guard will revisit their past words and actions over and over again, in a desperate need not to have done the 'wrong' thing. Their OCD in Fear Guard is, again, internal and provokes chants or counting in their heads, often the rituals of choice.

The Displaced Homebody exists in a state of shame.

Feeling like a failure for not saving others, they turn on themselves. Unable to fulfill their perceived purpose, they wonder why they exist at all? This creates a maladaptive telling of their story. They may cut and burn themselves to experience existence and to release pain. They may reject food and emaciate themselves through eating dis-orders.

The Homebody in Fear Guard attempts to go unseen by others, yet symbolically may literally write their stories on their bodies. Frozen thoughts mark their bodies, symbolizing the empathy they wish to create for others.

WALKABOUT

When Displaced Hunters feel shame they first blame others

When Displaced Homebodies feel shame they first blame themselves

THE DISPLACED HOMEBODY STORY

I was 22 when we had the fire. My parents were away that night and I had just put my little sister to bed. Our dog, Sassy, was scratching at the basement door; he usually slept down there at night, but was not ready to go to bed. I was really tired and I remember yelling at the dog to go to his bed. I grabbed a blanket and headed for the couch, too tired to do the dishes from the hot chocolate and popcorn we'd had. 'I will do them later' I said in my head.

Frantic barking woke me up. I thought I hadn't opened my eyes, it was so dark with smoke. I could hear my sister crying, she seemed close. I dropped to my knees and crawled, calling out for her. I am told that I was seen dragging her out the front door of the house. I don' remember. The next thing I remember is the smell of bleached hospital sheets and burnt hair.

Luckily my sister and Sassy got out ok. I had dragged my sister out and a neighbor had told the firefighters that we had a dog. They were able to get her out of the basement. In so many ways, Sassy saved all of us, but we lost everything else. Our home was gone.

The firefighter chief had told my parents that the fire had started with the stove being left on. I remember hearing that and shivering with fear. It was my fault. I had caused the fire. I was the reason we lost our home. I could not be trusted. I had not kept my family safe.

38 year old presenting with hoarding behaviour

NOTES

3

TribaLore: Darlene

Her whole life, Darlene loved the natural environment; she loved nature, animals, plants, lakes, ocean, sky and stars. She loved reading and fresh air. Knowing that she wanted to work outdoors and in nature from her earliest memory, Darlene attended University, studying forestry, and never returned to the city. She found work in her field in a forest community, where she met her husband. Together, they pursued their dreams and had the opportunity to buy a house on a large lake, with a sturdy dock and forty-eight stairs leading up to their three-bedroom house on an acre of land overlooking the lake. In her mid-late thirties, Darlene and her husband were blessed with three beautiful, healthy sons. The parents raised their sons in a loving family, sharing with them their love for the outdoors. They focused on physical activities, swimming, fishing, and boating. Each winter, her husband would build her sons a rink on the lake, and the boys grew up adoring their father and loved spending time with them. The boys excelled at soccer, baseball, and hockey.

"My husband was so involved with the kids. He taught them how to skate, and how to do their drills, and they loved it."

Darlene's son's athletic pursuits began to take them farther away as they grew older. As they switched schools to join more competitive teams, Darlene and her husband realized, to their shock, that drugs were being used and brought into their house by their sons. Their oldest son's drug issues escalated rapidly when he left for University. His personality began to change, he became depressed, and began talking about suicide. A drug-induced psychotic breakdown landed him in the hospital. Darlene and her husband were in disbelief when doctors explained that their eldest son had a severe drug dependency. As they worked towards getting their son accepted into a sober living house, their marriage began to suffer. With their two other sons beginning to engage in similarly disturbing behaviour, Darlene and her husband blamed themselves as parents. Neither had any of their immediate family nearby to provide support.

The day that her eldest son was admitted into a sober living home, the police came to Darlene's office to notify her that her husband had suffered a fatal cardiac arrest while exercising at the local recreation centre. He had been alone, unconscious for fourteen minutes before he was found deceased.

Now a single parent in a community without any family to support, Darlene first went on health leave and then resigned from her job as an administrator at a charity organization.

"My mom used to tell me to get my priorities straight. It didn't work out anymore with being a single mom and not having family here to assist my son. It just was not the right fit anymore."

Nearly two years after her husband's death, Darlene saw a three day Tribal Theory session on moral injury advertised through various mediums in her community. She googled Barb's background and decided it would be the right fit for her in addition to her bi-weekly counselling appointments. At the session, in attendance with 175 other people, Darlene purchased the first edition of this book and was drawn to Tribal Theory's framework and tools that could allow her to develop deeper understandings of her and her husband's spirit.

"I discovered that I am the Hunter; I couldn't wait to live this life. I couldn't wait to run away from my city dwelling life. My husband was the Homebody. His greatest sadness was not to be able to have his career right beside his family."

Tribal theory helped Darlene to understand that she needed more healing, and that this healing was not offered in conventional western psychiatry practices which encouraged her to go back to normal as quickly as possible.

"The way we deal with grief in our Western world was trying to pull me away from being my authentic self."

Like the blessings of finding her vocation in life, of meeting her husband, of having three kids later in life, and her beautiful home over a lake, Darlene considers finding Tribal Theory right when she needed it as a gift. She says that working with Barb and discovering the tools presented in this book have been key to her self understanding and growth. Tribal Theory has allowed her to validate her experiences. Her children have also started to learn about Tribal theory, and are using it to grow through their trauma.

"The fact that Tribal Theory just dropped into my lap is absolutely amazing. It's amazing."

TribaLORE: Doris

Doris was raised in a French Canadian home with seven children and a mother who wasn't capable of taking care of them, both emotionally and physically. Her dad worked long hours in a factory while an older brother ran the house. This brother was a cruel predator, who abused nearly everybody living in the house - physically, emotionally, and in some cases, sexually. Doris reported this abuse to her mother, who did not do anything about it. Half of her siblings still don't know it happened.

"I remember being seven and looking in the bathroom mirror and asking myself, 'what's going to happen to me?'. Something is really wrong here."

What began as cruelty when she was a child escalated when she became a preteen. Doris left her family home the day before her nineteenth birthday, but still remained in contact with her family for twenty years after, living in what she describes as a sort of Stockholm Syndrome state.

When she was forty, her sister attempted suicide and Doris went to a counsellor to learn how to best support her. This counsellor encouraged her to begin addressing her own trauma, which she did. She separated herself and her sister from most of their family, and life became relatively normal again. She met her husband with whom she traveled the world. She tried to enjoy her life.

Eight years ago, Doris' Father died. At his funeral, her abusive brother was sitting behind her.

"All I can remember from my father's funeral is being terrified as my brother was sitting directly behind me and I thought that I might have to give him the sign of peace. I can't go to funerals anymore. It was retraumatizing." Doris says of this experience.

Since that time, her mother also passed away. Doris' husband was diagnosed with Alzheimer's, and she became legally blind. She continued to carry trauma from her father's funeral. Her life began to unravel.

"I was stuck, frozen, in a hole."

One of Doris' counsellors encouraged her to begin working with the Tribal Theory framework. Doris was drawn to the method's adaptability, relevance to her own experience, and compassionate, spiritual foundation. She struggled with the framework at first.

"My Fear Guard was so high that I couldn't even understand what a fear guard was.", she explains.

Slowly, Tribal Theory has allowed Doris to take her fragmented thoughts and recollections and to stitch them together. She says she no longer feels like an outcast.

"Tribal Theory was a framework that helped me make meaning of my story. I was able to re-write my story understanding that my authentic gifts in Fear Guard, generalized anxiety and depression, were trying to tell the story of what happened to me. Once I understood this, I could start to make changes and nurture my authentic self.

WALKABOUT

The displaced Homebody will question their self-worth

The displaced Hunter will lose their self-esteem

WALKABOUT

Using EVOKE instead of TRIGGER

"As soon as I changed from using the word trigger to using the word evoke, I felt like my cells were dancing with joy, I could begin to heal from the inside, it wasn't about 'out there' anymore"

25 year old female, sexually assaulted at the age of 14

The term trigger implies that you are responding to something 'outside' of yourself, something you have no control of, an 'out of the blue' thing that has provoked you, something familiar. It provokes feelings associated with a trauma response. The very use of the word 'trigger' may require our amygdala to be on constant guard, hypervigilant, consistently scanning and scoping in an effort to prepare for the unpreparable.

Tribal Theory suggests that the term 'trigger' be replaced with the term 'evoke'. Evoke is from the inside out. It gives one the opportunity to prepare and start to take responsibility for how they respond. Knowing they are evoked because of their story, one can make meaning of their response rather than waiting to respond on instinct or impulse alone.

There are many limitations in social work and counselling in efforts not to 'trigger', retraumatized individuals. It is nearly impossible to consistently avoid sights, sounds, and words that trigger individuals. Using the term evoke, a person may acknowledge and identify that this is a unique, personal reaction, allowing them to feel less like a victim, and to begin to understand that it is an internal response that they can begin to manage.

Consider these two sentences.

I was so triggered by that scene in the movie last night.

The scene in the movie last night was evocative.

Can you feel a shift?

WALKABOUT

THE SHOULDERING OF SHOULD

A word commonly found throughout trauma narratives is 'should'.

When one is told or tells oneself that they 'should' have done something, they often respond with an uncomfortable twinge. The term 'should' implies that they did wrong; they could have done better; they made a poor choice; that it is time to doubt themself; they are looking bad in front of others. 'Shoulds' create an infinite feedback loop of judgement, criticism, and self-blame. Imagine this word and imagine how it can evoke the cellular memory of those who have grown up or are now experiencing a hyper-critical home or environment.

There are some people who are more sensitive to the spoken word than others. It may be that through their experiences, their response is the result of past criticism It is possible that they may have experienced little else.

The use of this word impacts our belief in our abilities; it evokes doubt. It is a word that can make us feel like failures and creates a sense of fragility. It renounces our strength in being.

Should evokes blame; could evokes strength.

THE CHANGING OF THE GUARD
Healthy Guard Guide
To
Fear Guard Protector

THE CHANGING OF THE GUARD
THE HYPERVIGILANT PROTECTOR IN FEAR GUARD

As the Healthy Guard turns into Fear Guard, the Protector turns into a Hypervigilant Protector. This manifests the gifts of the Hunter and Homebody into maladaptive behaviours.

Tribal Theory sees these behaviours as a response to dis-placement, dis-ease, and dis-order. In understanding these responses, consider taking away the prefix of these three words and you will note that the Healthy Guard is responsible for placement, ease, and order, always waiting in the wings.

So let's consider a few maladaptive behaviours that again, are Genius gifts, transformed while responding in Fear Guard.

O C D

MAGICAL THINKING

Only Caring & Daring
(& Daring to Care)

PROTECTING USING MAGICAL THINKING

THE MAGICAL BRAIN

"you can't tame the Spirit of someone who has Magic in their veins."   - Unknown

A Caring & Daring Hunter's Story

I always ran, skipped or jumped as a kid. I was told by my family that I would grab my pillow and blanket and sneak out to our back covered porch on summer nights to sleep, and climbing trees made me feel good. One summer

evening when I was ten, I was in the backyard digging for something, I don't remember what, when I heard my father yelling, so loud, the loudest I have ever heard anyone yell before. Then a big smash and my little brother's voice screaming "don't, don't Dad, don't", followed by another smash. I don't remember how I got in the house, but I must have ran. I remember almost slipping on our kitchen floor and grabbing the corner of the counter. As I steadied myself I saw my Dad, blood on his hands and broken glass everywhere. I turned and my little brother was curled up in the corner of the room, his hands over his head, his whole body shaking. I saw what had happened. There was the television set, the screen shattered, a bottle sticking out of the screen like it had pierced through from the back of the console. I remember thinking how it looked like a front of a ship, poking through ice. I turned and saw Dad, slouched, as he mumbled something and turned to walk out of the room. He stopped by the entryway and for a moment seemed calm. Then, he punched the wall so hard his fist went through it. His arm got stuck, and I wanted to help him, but I was too scared, was afraid he would hit me. He looked at me, his eyes so dark, said "forget this crap", and he went out our front door. I went towards my brother, who was still shaking, leaned down to put my arms around him and help him up and as I leaned down, I saw my mother hiding behind the couch. She looked at me. I had never seen her scared, but she looked both frightened and frightening. I have to take care of everyone, I thought. Mom can't do it right now. And it was that night, after I got my little brother to bed, reading him his favourite story, after putting a blanket on my Mom as she fell asleep in her clothes in the big recliner chair, that I went and locked all the doors and windows in the house, scared that my Dad would return the same monster he was when he left. It was that night that I checked the doors and windows three times each. Because I knew there were only three of us now, and I had to keep our home safe from him.

14 year old girl with outward OCD

We know that around nine to twelve years of age, the magical thinking, once the creative part of a child's brain, shifts. If a child has had the opportunity to be in and know their authentic self, this magical thinking develops into healthy creative thought and exploration. Artistic and scientific minds flourish given the space to do so; magic and creative minds go full throttle.

If a child is displaced in Fear Guard, this magical thinking can turn into 'what if' thinking (in Homebodies) or 'thinking the worst first' (in Hunters). It still shifts into creative thought and exploration, but it is not in joy or curiosity, but survival and caution. This presents itself as OCD, the acronym in Tribal Theory for Only Caring and Daring (and Daring to Care). This acronym is also identifiable as representing Obsessive Compulsive Disorder. Let's look at this disorder from a displacement framework.

Look at our young girl again. We know that she has been pushed into a Homebody role to protect other family members. She is no longer supported to explore and learn. Not able to be in her authentic role, she may have tried to use her magical thinking to imagine escape routes, visualize a peaceful place she could take her siblings, or even create an imaginary friend to take care of. As she turns nine, her brain and body, in constant Fear Guard, usurp that magical thinking and, instead of developing into joyous creativity, uses it to create magical rituals to keep others and herself safe.

The Fear Guard uses magical thinking and turns it into obsessive thoughts and compulsive behaviour, ways to creatively react in order to keep others safe. OCD develops in order to keep oneself or others safe. "If I tap my toe three times on the school desk leg before I go home, my Dad will not try to come back tonight; if my stuffed animals are in a certain order around my head, on my pillow, my Mom will not die; if I do the same routine every day before I go to sleep, everyone will be safe, no harm will come in the night, no one will die."

Obsessive and compulsive behaviour is an attempt to keep yourself and others safe.

If used by the authentic self and the Healthy Guard, this is a gift. It is a disorder, a caring and daring one, if used in Fear Guard.

A Daring to Care Homebody Story

It happened so fast. I was sitting in the back of our car watching the raindrops racing each other on the back window. I remember rooting for the tinier drop. Then we were spinning, the whole car, lights swirling around us, a huge red one seemed to follow me like the eye of a monster. Then a heavy feeling on my chest. The moving stopped. I remember I saw the top of my mother's head. Her hair stuck to the roof of the car like it had been glued. I couldn't breathe. I heard sirens. After that I remember a firm but kind voice telling me I was going to be okay. You and your Mom are okay. I wanted to believe that voice.

For a year after that, anytime I saw anyone get in a car, I felt that if I didn't say a quick prayer, something bad would happen to them and it would be my fault. I only do it if it is a red car now. That was the colour of our car that was in the accident, and I only say 'bless you', so it is better.

As far as riding in a car, I refuse to sit in the back. I have to sit in the front, and each time we come to a red light, I look and if someone is standing at the corner waiting to cross I say 'you believe' in my head.

24 year old with inward OCD

MAGICAL THINKING -THE HUNTER IN FEAR GUARD

Because Hunters are naturally outward bound, they will present OCD behaviours outwardly. Their OCD is transparent. It may involve shutting cupboards three times, washing hands over and over, or checking and rechecking doors and checking again. The Hunters fear that if they don't check and abide by this ritual someone they care about will be hurt or die.

MAGICAL THINKING -THE HOMEBODY IN FEAR GUARD

Homebodies are internally focused. They will present with OCD behaviours that can't be seen - inner thoughts that stay in hiding. Persistent thoughts; mantras; chants; imagining that they may have hurt someone and not letting go of that fear; re-living a part of the day when they interacted with someone, self-consciously going over the conversation hoping they did not say anything wrong. These rituals are to make sure they do not hurt others or cause someone to die.

ANXIETY

ANXIETY & FEAR GUARD

We live in a fear-based culture, wherein the Authentic Hunter and Homebody are no longer able to carry out their roles in the Tribe. They are overwhelmed with the belief that they have to be in Fear Guard at all times. This constant feeling of fear overstimulates the amygdala. With no resting time to create safety, the Fear Guard remains in charge. Coping skills now become maladaptive as they try to work in a heightened mental & physical fear state.

Fear Guard anxiety is processed and presented differently in the Hunter and the Homebody.

ANXIETY -THE HUNTER IN FEAR GUARD

THINKING THE WORST FIRST

Anxiety comes and goes for a Hunter and is more about a loss of control in their outer environment.

It presents as a need to control others, specific phobias such as fear of heights and flying (no control), and panic attacks.

When a Hunter has a panic attack, along with general symptoms, the feeling of being 'out of body' is predominant.

ANXIETY -THE HOMEBODY IN FEAR GUARD

MY AMYGDALA NEVER SLEEPS

Anxiety for a Homebody is anxiety that they carry inside of themselves.

It presents as social anxiety, social phobia, and generalized anxiety with panic attacks.

When a Homebody has a panic attack, the feeling of not being able to create an inner calm is predominant.

NOTES

HOME
IS WHERE
THE HOARD (HEART) IS

When a Homebody feels that they are not protecting others, their magical thinking, OCD, can present as hoarding. Through hoarding, everything holds a symbolic message of, 'you never know when you might need it'. By holding onto things (many use the term 'packrat'), we are keeping (packing) things in preparation for the next terrible thing that might happen.

The Homebody clutters with care and 'feels' their tangible things. Homebodies are natural collectors of items, but when displaced, or having experienced cumulative trauma, they can respond with maladaptive collecting and their anxiety increases if they are asked to 'let go' of anything.

THE HOMEBODY'S CARING HEART BEHIND HOARDING
AN ILLUSTRATION AND CONSIDERATION

A stay-at-home mother was raising four young children. Her husband, a soldier, had died in war. The husband was an Authentic Hunter and the mother an Authentic Homebody. After the husband's death, the mother, with support, was able to work outside the home to keep a living income, and continue to provide a comforting home, a safe place for them to heal and grow. A few years later the oldest son, age 10, got leukemia and, though, medically, everything was put in place, he died. The mother who had been able to endure the loss of her husband and to take on both roles to provide for her children, took the death of her son as a penance, and felt that she had neglected her children by working outside the home. She felt that had she been home more, she would have seen the signs of illness, and been able to provide more nutritious meals. The guilt of not being there consumed her. She was displaced by her husband's death, and forced into a Hunter role unable to accept why she had to work, she did not make meaning of her loss. Now, with another loss, and still unable to make meaning, and feeling shamed, she took the blame and created the story that it was her fault. She began to hold on to everything, and her guilt, shame and blame presented itself as hoarding.

THE OUT of CONTROL

When a Hunter feels that they are not providing or protecting others, their magical thinking, OCD, can present as over-controlling behaviour. For them, in order to get things 'under control', to stop other things from going 'wrong', there is a certain place and way to do everything. This is often imposed on others as well. The Hunter will ask themselves and others to follow their 'rules of engagement'. These may include the 'proper way' of doing and being. Strict requirements like how one talks, stands, engages in activities are enforced, observed, and ridiculed. There is an established way to cook, clean, dress, and interact with people.

The Hunter's OCD is like insignia, stripes on the shoulder of a sergeant. This is an armed and ready strategy. This is meant to show and tell others that you are a warrior primed and ready to keep the enemy at bay. It creates a sense of control as Hunter's think the worst first, and work backwards to mitigate something bad happening.

DEPRESSION
The Symptom of Oppression

The carrying of unjust treatment or prolonged moral injury after being subject to control and a lack of emotional justice has a profoundly oppressive impact on our body, mind & spirit, on the essence of who we are meant to be. The Genius presents this oppression as Depression.

This is the place where both Hunter & Homebody present with many of the same characteristics. Yet, it is often easier to observe the changes in the Hunter as they were once more outgoing, whereas the Homebody, more internal, is not as 'seen'.

ADDICTIONS

Addictions present to cope with trauma. They are signs of a spiritual crisis, a yearning to find one's authentic self, place and purpose. They are an effort to try and reach, touch, taste, and feel the authentic self when displaced.

Most addictions develop from the moral injury of the accumulated injustices that have happened to someone. The constant requirement to be in Fear Guard Protector creates an 'addict' where one is actually 'addicted' to finding meaning in order to survive.

SELF HARM
THE PRACTICE OF SPIRITUAL HEALING

"I feel like a ghost until I feel the sting and the warmth then I think maybe I am me"

17 year old who 'cuts'

Displaced Hunters and displaced Homebodies use self-harm to try and move from displacement. It is a symbol of spiritual crisis, and the ritual of a 'lost soul'. The cellular pain that they experience evokes primal gestures like cutting, burning, and bone breaking to try and connect with their soul.

Tribal Theory provides an alternative approach to addressing and understanding non-suicidal self-injury.

Using the framework to acknowledge the story of how the soul was misplaced, in present time or in preceding generations, it allows individuals to re-tell their story. In doing so, the soul is awakened, as it was never lost.

WALKABOUT

DIS-order	ORDER
DIS-ease	EASE
DIS-placed	PLACE

WALKABOUT

Once you see that healing is about being in your authentic 'place,' it is like pulling a thread. You know that something is happening. There is a baseline shift, a ripple effect, and the meaning of that shift infiltrates all of the stories of who you are and what happened to you. It re-aligns the whole story - the thread becomes a lifeline.

RESILIENCE

"Challenging the meaning of life is the truest expression of the state of being human" - Victor Frankl

WHAT ABOUT RESILIENCE?

A pivotal characteristic of Tribal Theory is its capacity to evolve within its own framework as it combines the experience and knowledge of others with my own. The term resilience, when used to describe the trauma-mitigating function of coping mechanisms, has always made me uncomfortable. Can resilience resolve a traumatic response? Resilience is defined as 'the ability of a substance or object to bounce back' or 'the capacity to recover quickly from toughness or difficulties'. Trauma is not a dead-end street that one can back out of to return to the main road. Trauma is a moral injury that disrupts the life flow of both body and spirit; there is no road back, the main road is no longer accessible.

Well-intentioned concepts and strategies of swift recovery from trauma are profoundly incomplete. Moral injury, much like chronic physical pain, requires ongoing treatment and healing trauma is a holistic spiritual endeavor. Trauma, which shapes our self-understanding, can be a lifelong burden if it is inadequately addressed. However, through Sensory Dialogue, Symbolics, and Timeless Travel, trauma can become a portal to meaningful, enriching, and empowering self-understanding.

Tribal theory invites us to explore and re-envision who we are, where we belong, and our authentic role. It reveals safely how we have responded to trauma and, through telling our experiences being witnessed and believed, to recognize our moral injury. By making meaning of trauma, Tribal Theory offers a way to move forward. Its emphasis is not recovery. Its emphasis is integration, regeneration, and evolution.

Many psychologists construct resilience as the process of an individual adapting well in the aftermath of adversity, crisis, tragedy, trauma, threats, or stress. Adapting, however, is not the same as making meaning and integrating. How does one adapt when the very nature of trauma is unexpected chaos and hurt, often followed by years of basic survival? Trauma produces a protective response which itself takes time to heal. This response bypasses our own fragmented cognition of what has happened, and then lives in us. The body remembers.

Moral injury cannot be prepared for but, once it has happened, it can be identified and meaning can be made of it. Then, and only then, can the body feel safe again. Addressing trauma via the framework of psychology - a behavioural framework - compromises one's healing potential. A moral injury can only be healed through addressing and subsequently evolving a person's core sacred beliefs. Through this approach, we can integrate our experiences into our story, and evolve our understanding of our fundamental nature, reality, and existence. Resilience programs that focus on cognitive therapy can be helpful in developing coping methods for stress in adverse situations, but not for trauma.

The body responds very differently to trauma than crisis. Treating trauma with cognitive therapy is like using penicillin to stop the spread of a cancer. A moral injury is a force of its own and 'penicillin' will not work. As noted earlier in this book, systems of narrative and cognitive therapy do little to shift cellular trauma. We cannot build emotional resilience to trauma. We need to integrate and make meaning of what has happened and in doing so, we do not recover, we evolve.

Trauma cannot be avoided or mitigated, nor can its impact be lessened through the training of the mind through resiliency programs. While resiliency programs may be helpful in learning coping skills for everyday adversity and crisis, their inability to identify trauma as moral injury can cause further spiritual crises. This, in turn, can lead to magnified feelings of displacement, alienation, and 'deaths of despair', which include drug poisonings, suicide, and alcohol-induced death.

Once again, emotional trauma is a moral injury in need of soul repair. It is healed when this is recognized, integrated and addressed through the pillars of the spiritual, cultural, physical and philosophical. To heal trauma, western behavioural psychology procedures need not only to be out of sight, but out of mind.

WHAT ABOUT CHILDREN?

A child who has been able to explore and develop their authentic self will build a strong sense of self-worth and self-esteem. With the addition of healthy nurturing, a second advantage is realized; the gift of making meaning. Why is nurturing so important? As a child explores their authentic self, they are guided by nature, whether they are a Hunter, rolling in the dirt, tasting ants, climbing objects, or a Homebody, building bed sheet forts, sorting and placing stuffed animals, helping to cook. If a child makes a mistake while taking on these natural draws, a nurturing caregiver will not criticize. They will turn it into a learning moment. This acceptance encourages a child to become confident in their natural interests and abilities and to know that they can problem solve and resolve when making mistakes.

What if that child is not allowed to grow in their authentic role? What if the child is not nurtured, but criticized, shamed, or blamed? This child has a lesser chance of developing resilience because this child lives in the position of the Fear Guard.

This place is where children feel like 'misfits', 'castaways', or 'lost'. They have little, if any, integration or ability to make meaning of challenges because anytime they have tried to solve a problem, criticism has made them feel like failures. They don't believe that they can 'weather the storm,' and all too often feel they are actually the cause of it.

The body remembers and it can feel like the spirit has disappeared or been lost. Without the spirit to guide the authentic self the child does not get over it or bounce back. The child lives 'in' it.

I am often asked about children who are able to be in their authentic role and not criticized, yet who are also not given healthy instructions on how to resolve mistakes or problems, and who are left to their own devices. These children will do well on the outside, yet consistently seek validation in relationships, presenting as strong individuals but feeling lost without the acknowledgment of others.

This is difficult for the authentic self because it has learned to 'doubt', and this, in turn, can lead to difficulties in decision making.

Nevertheless, even after years of not being able to be one's authentic self and/or not being granted the gift of resilience through external nurturing, the simple action of identifying one's authentic self and understanding that one was pushed or forced into a Fear Guard position can create a paradigm shift in how one sees themselves and the world. One can then begin taking steps towards healing and well-being.

THE SENSE-ABLE STORY

Sometimes, you may be baffled because you cannot recall anything traumatic that has happened to you. You may believe that you were fortunate to have a healthy family and/or community environment which supported your growth and that you have made meaning of adverse events in your life, yet you still feel dis-placed.

This is when asking yourself about your birth, childhood illnesses, or events that happened before you could talk (from your non-verbal years) can be helpful as you may have a 'sense-able' story to tell. These trauma responses are imprinted in your sensory memory and can prove enlightening as you may not have considered the possible impact of these events. You will carry these events as sensory responses. You had no words to cognitively tell the story of what happened, but your senses can tell and keep the story in the cells all over your body (this is often referred to as cellular memory) .

When one is able to attach 'sense' responses to experiences, and then to a narrative, one's seemingly impulsive responses are no longer impulsive and they will be 'able' to make meaning of their story.

Tribal Theory calls it the '**sense able**' story.

"So maybe this is why I feel this way around needles and get a headache and panicky whenever I even think about them."

16 year old who was hospitalized for the first three months of their life as a preemie and gets anxious and has panic attacks when walking past clinics or hospitals.

NOTES

MORAL INJURY

MORAL INJURY

"Emotional Trauma is Moral Injury in need of Soul Repair"

– B. Allyn

Tribal Theory presents four core foundational pillars which integrate crisis, adversity, and trauma in order to provide individuals with a new perspective that includes purpose, meaning, and belonging. These four pillars are Spiritual, Cultural, Physical, and Philosophical.

In Tribal Theory, the Spiritual Pillar refers to an individual's core beliefs through which they derive solace and meaning. The Cultural Pillar describes the lens through which one perceives this world, and how historic tribal and family roots have shaped one's view. The Physical Pillar is the body's health, determined by one's access to the physical resources required to adequately nurture and enhance their mind-body connection. The Philosophical Pillar is an individual's expression of their core values, how they discover symbolic meaning.

Notably, psychology is not one of the four pillars.

Trauma assessments in contemporary Western psychology are deeply rooted in arcane Western constructions of normalcy, justifiable behaviour, and the human consciousness. While these beliefs continue to direct and shape psychiatric thinking and practices around the globe, the western lens is not a global one.

One of the founders of modern psychology, and the first person to refer to themself as a psychologist, was Wilhelm Maximillian Wundt (1820 to 1832). Also a physician, physiologist, philosopher, and professor, Wundt believed that the existence of a soul was irrelevant to psychological learning, as individuals could only be understood in physical terms. In the late 17th century, as psychology began to be studied in universities, it became known as the study of 'the spirit which denied the spirit'.

Tribal Theory argues that this heavy-handed Western focus on psychology, developed from a framework which neglects the spirit, continues to impose its biased definition on the world - a world without spirit - and has resulted in a permeating western perspective. This perspective excludes organic, historic, and tribal healing practices of other belief systems, to the detriment of all (including the west).

Tribal Theory holds the belief that there is no pre or post-trauma. Trauma is trauma. Until trauma is experienced, processed, and an individual has developed a sense of belonging with others who have experienced it, trauma can not be meaningfully understood and integrated into one's self-knowledge. One's spiritual connection to themselves and others will be disconnections, leading to despair. Trauma is a Moral Injury. In order to heal trauma, the Spiritual Pillar must be addressed first, followed by the Cultural, Physical, and lastly Philosophical. Psychology, founded on the denial of the spirit, will not heal Moral Injury - it will hinder healing.

Tribal Theory first bears witness to the individual and what has happened to them, without labelling and pathologizing them. This framework creates a safe place for people to share their core beliefs, to sit with their body remembering, and to hear the unique story of each soul. No matter how many times someone verbally shares their response to trauma; until they can make meaning of what has happened to them, the shame and spiritual anguish will be further embedded by each retelling of the story.

TRIBAL THEORY - THE FOUR PILLARS OF MORAL INJURY

Below are illustrations of the four Pillars of Tribal Theory as they are used to commence the exploration of moral injury. Each Pillar requires attention; they lay the foundation for each person's unique story. Within this supportive framework, the storyteller is empowered to become the story-maker, unearthing the spiritual and symbolic meaning of what happened to them and how they can integrate it into their self-knowledge. As trauma is transformed into a story of crisis followed by adversity, each of the foundational Pillars are strengthened as the individual evolves spiritually, culturally, physically, and philosophically.

Draw these four Pillars and name each one as illustrated below. Begin with the Spiritual Pillar and write or converse with another person regarding how you identify within each Piller. How do you define your spirit? What is your cultural identity? How is your physical health? What is your philosophy? These pillars construct your story.

Now, take what happened to you, the event(s) you hold as trauma, and see where and how they impacted your story.

Understanding how events have shaped your pillars - your story - you will begin to understand why you continue to carry the trauma. You will begin to make meaning. Your moral injury will become your story of adversity and crisis, your path of seasoned knowledge, your inner wisdom, your strength, your spirit.

TRIBAL THEORY - THE FOUR PILLARS

SPIRITUAL   CULTURAL   PHYSICAL   PHILOSOPHICAL

The HEALING PRACTICES of Tribal Theory

The Trauma Life Line
Timeless Travel
Sensory Dialogue
Symbolics

THE HEALING PRACTICES OF TRIBAL THEORY

"The cave you fear to enter holds the treasure you seek"

Joseph Campbell

As Tribal Theory evolved, I developed practices to help individuals uncover and explore their authentic place in the Tribe and to begin to identify and unravel the events and circumstances of their past. The experiences that had most significantly shaped their life choices and consequent outcomes.

These simple methods have proven to be very powerful in this respect and they work in tandem to reveal valuable insights that in and of themselves often prove to be helpfully transformative.

THE TRAUMA LIFE LINE

HOW TO CREATE THE TRAUMA LIFE LINE

The easiest way to illustrate and understand these tools is to apply them to your own life story.

1. On a piece of blank paper, in the landscape position, draw a single straight line across the paper from left to right, about 1/3 of the way from the top.
2. Label this line the 'Healthy Guard Guide'.
3. Draw a second straight line across the paper from left to right, parallel to the first line and about 2/3rds of the way from the top.
4. Label this line the 'Fear Guide Protector"
5. Draw a third straight line across the paper from left to right, parallel to the first line and about 2/3rds of the way from the second line
6. Label this line the 'Trauma Life Line'
7. Write 'birth' on the left and 'now' on the right of each of these lines.

Healthy Guard - Guide

birth_____now

Fear Guard - Protector
birth_____now

Trauma Life Line

birth_____now

USING THE TRAUMA LIFE LINE

The Trauma Life Line is where we are asked to tell our unique story. In Tribal Theory, these are the answers to the who, what, where, and why questions. Who do you think hurt you? What did you do to survive? Where did you feel safe? When did you start guarding yourself and others? Once you see the Why, it will be time to change your story.

Starting with the Trauma LifeLine, try to remember experiences or events in your life that seemed to have a disruptive or negative impact on you or that you would consider as a crisis or traumatic event.

Write a short label or phrase that represents the experience on the Trauma Life Line at the place that most closely represents the age in your life (between your birth and now) when this experience, or these experiences, occurred.

Continue identifying and marking events where you responded traumatically on the Trauma Life Line until you are satisfied that you have recorded the 'main events' that you can remember at this point in time. Don't worry about the neatness or any specific order.

This is more of a jam session than a recording session.

You are encouraged to use **Sensory Dialogue** and **Symbolics,** which are described in the next chapters of this book, while developing your trauma life line. If you have no words to describe events on your line, Identify where on your timeline **senses** and **symbols** are **evoked.**

The Trauma Life Line is a way to assist you in telling 'your' story about the challenging events that have had adverse effects on your life. It becomes a 'safe place' for you to monograph your experiences and it can be helpful whether or not you have yet identified with an Authentic Tribal role. Many times, in fact, it may help you to discover and clarify what your role is likely to be. The Trauma Life Line is a line of self-inquiry that emerges from the inside out. Because you are recalling and recreating your own story, you will uncover and express what you want or innately need to reveal.

(Note for those of you counseling clients. They may find identifying with one event is enough in your session with them. You can always pick it up where you left off next time you see them or they can take it with them and add on when they are ready.)

THE HEALTHY GUARD (GUIDE) & THE FEAR GUARD (PROTECTOR)

The Healthy Guard and Fear Guard Lines help to reveal an alternative story. They illustrate the Genius in all of us that was called upon to find creative ways to survive when our lives or safety were threatened by someone or something in our past.

In Tribal Theory, making meaning, connection, safety and belonging are foundational healing from crisis and growing in trauma. As you consider the different trauma responses to events identified on the Trauma Life Line use the parallel lines to consider and mark how your Authentic self, along with the Healthy Guard Guide gifts, had to go into Fear Guard Protector to try to protect you in your times of need.

This is where you can shift the Trauma Life Line story into one of caring, bravery, and genius. As you see how you were able to call on your Healthy Guard gifts to guide you and it shape shifted into a hypervigilant Fear Guard Protector to creatively try and protect you through difficult and challenging times, you will simultaneously begin to write a new story of how you did the best you could under the circumstances.

Working through this guideline process, we gain a greater understanding of how connection is so very important to us as humans. Tribal Theory suggests that it is very difficult, if not impossible, to connect in a healthy and productive way with ourselves and others or to make meaning of what has happened if we are dis-placed. Understanding the Fear Guard Protector helps our amygdala to calm down and in turn the rest of our body. Our cellular memory is witnessed. One is able to make more meaning of what happened to them. A paradigm shift occurs that changes your life story.

Every mark on the Trauma Life Line is a chapter in your story, a bread crumb marking a trail, acknowledging and validating your experiences. It is an opportunity to gain insight into what actually has happened to you and will help you make sense of your dis-order, dis-ease, and feelings of dis-placement. It will help you to step back with order, ease and placement and to look at your life.

Victims become survivors and a survivor can thrive as they self-identify with their new story and their Authentic role in the Tribe.

THE HOMEBODY
Illustration & Consideration

There is a young man in his early 30's who finds it difficult to go back to work after a flood that occurred in his office. It happened in the basement of the building where he works and his office is on the first floor. When the flood happened he and other co-workers evacuated the building and no one was hurt, or, in the man's perception, was bothered much by it. However, when he went to return to work he found that as soon as he got close to the building he experienced a panic attack. He felt he could not breathe, his teeth clenched and he felt disconnected. These panic feelings continued to happen each day for several days and so he went to the hospital. He was diagnosed with anxiety and it was suggested he consider counselling.

This man identified as an Authentic Homebody. While doing his Trauma Life line, he related different things that he had encountered that he considered traumatic. He started relating stories about his adolescent years and then suddenly lowered his voice and whispered that, during his childhood, around the age of seven, his mother had been in a car accident. I asked if he would be comfortable talking about it further. He continued, now in his normal tone, and said that it had left his mother physically disabled and immobile. She started drinking heavily. He said they lived in a rancher house, with no upstairs, just a basement. When she would drink, his mother would get very angry and yell a lot. His father, after a couple of years of trying to understand his mother's frustration and drinking to feel better, would often not come home from work until she had passed out from drinking. This left him, as a boy, to come home from school to take care and deal with his mother's emotional outbursts. He told the story about how he would go to the basement, which was always damp, and hide. Telling his mother he was going out to be with friends, but knowing he could not leave her alone, he would go to the basement with comics and a flashlight. He could hear his mother above, so he would be aware if she fell or hurt herself. He felt scared at times, but also felt it was the right thing to do.

By telling the story and now being aware of his sensory memories, he connected the smells of the basement with the flood at work. It had evoked the feelings he felt when he had to be so quiet in the basement, in the dark, scared for his mother and always paying attention to every little noise, in case the 'stranger', as he referred to his mother when she was intoxicated, came alive in the house. He began to connect his physiological responses to his cellular memories of being pushed into the Fear Guard role; a Homebody with no safe place or ability to create one. The flood had literally brought a 'flood' of memories to the surface. He had found meaning in his panic attacks.

In drawing the Healthy Guard Guide and Fear Guard Protector over his Trauma Life Line he was able to look at what his Authentic Guide had been doing. He discovered that his authentic guide within himself had a caring, understanding and empathetic nature.

As a young boy, he had tried to care for his mother, and

understood that his father had to stay away. This included, empathizing with his mother's loss of mobility in the car accident, empathy for his father's loss of a partner and an awareness of his own innate bravery in coming forth and doing his best, while displaced, to take care of the situation.

He went on further to connect this displacement with the maladaptive behaviours that surfaced in his adolescense.

His panic attacks subsided and he returned to work.

NOTES

TribaLORE: Amy

Amy grew up in Ontario in a loving and supportive family. Her younger brother, the middle sibling, was diagnosed with cancer as a child.

"My parents did a really good job of including us in that experience. They protected us when they needed to, but also made us aware of the realities of the situation. We had special rules in our house because of my brother's condition. They got us a family membership at the Toronto zoo so that when we had to travel to Sick Kids in Toronto, we could also take a family trip."

After three years of chemo, Amy's brother went into remission. Life momentarily went back to normal and Amy began high school. Sadly, it was not long until the doctors discovered that her brother's cancer had returned and he needed a bone marrow transplant. Amy was a match, and donated bone marrow to her brother. The transplant worked, but her brother didn't survive. Amy was fifteen years old.

"I didn't ever really see this as a real source of trauma until I realized, much later, that this had formed entire parts of my sense of self and who I became in life."

Amy struggled as a teenager to fit in. She skipped class, but always managed to receive fantastic grades despite putting in the minimum effort. She went to college, became a social worker, and started working in group homes. She began a relationship with a man, and very quickly had two daughters within 18 months. This relationship turned out to be a significant source of trauma and moral injury.

When Amy used the framework of Tribal Theory it made so much sense. Especially the concept of how her authentic self had tried to protect her brother and had felt a sense of failure when she could not. She became aware that she had honed her authentic Homebody trying to care for her brother yet was left with a sense of low self worth. She would carry these experiences into her future and dedicate herself, often neglecting her own needs, to help others feel better.

Amy identified as a Homebody, and now understood that after leaving her abusive relationship, she had also been forced out of her Homebody role and into her Fear Guard in order to protect her daughters. She then began piece-by-piece to get back to a safe place and back into her authentic self.

"I felt completely out of sorts and chaotic, like nothing fit. I finally had my aha moment! I understood that these experiences were something that happened to me, not that something is wrong with me. I have my own natural gifts to help me heal."

NOTES

WALKABOUT

Many of our childhood memories about ourselves come from other people's stories. We often carry these stories and believe them to be the true reflection of who we are. However, they may not be.

Tales told to us of our strengths, gifts and wisdom shape us differently than those pointing out our weakness, failures and lack of awareness.

The stories told to us, about us, by others, can have a strong influence on how we began and continue to perceive ourselves.

TIMELESS TRAVEL

Trauma response activates the survival instinct which then impedes sequential cognitive recollection. What remains after trauma is fragmented thought, like the scattered pieces of a puzzle. While the body remembers an event by storing it in its senses and its cells, the brain is essentially in a time warp. Tribal Theory calls this response Timeless Travel.

As a traumatic event, and the response it evoked, fades into the past, a person is still left with fragmented memory. With no clear sense of time, an interruption of normal linear thought, and confusing overlapping memories, it can feel as though one is living displaced and disconnected in an alternate reality. Visual images, flashbacks, and a sense of doom often accompany this. Consider the difference between a dream and a night terror. A strange dream might leave one asking questions and seeking meaning. A night terror evokes haunting panic. After responding to a crisis, there is a return to a logical and true sequential memory. Adversity may evoke bad dreams, but with trauma, terror waits around every corner. Trauma response produces Timeless Travel. This disorientation can subsequently lead to individuals being labelled as disordered or mentally ill. Reacting to moral injury, travelling in the timeless space produced by trauma - a space they go until they can make meaning of their experience - these labels cause further harm.

Example

A woman in her thirties volunteered in a hospital, inspired by another volunteer who, a few years earlier, had helped her mother in aftercare following a difficult surgery. This individual had sat with her mother, telling stories about a shelter for animals that her father ran and the adventures that ensued. The young woman's mother loved animals and would beam listening to the stories of rescue and healing. The mother later passed under tragic circumstances; trapped in a house fire, wheelchair bound, she could not be saved.

The young woman attended grief counselling to deal with her loss. After her mother's death, she became unprecedentedly and inexplicably fearful of animals, and this fear progressed until the young woman became nearly housebound, afraid to venture outside and be confronted by a squirrel or a dog. It progressed until she could not watch any nature shows on television and she lived in constant fear. She was no longer volunteering. Traumatized, the young woman came to me for support.

I got to know the young woman and the reason she had pursued volunteering. When she spoke of how her mother had seemed to have healed from surgery because of the animal rescue stories, timeless travel presented itself.

In short, the young women had overlapped the animal rescue stories and the healing that had once helped her mother with the tragic incident of her mother's death and the grief and shame she experienced when she had been unable to save her. This timeless travel fused the two stories together where they held trauma. The young woman's belief that the animal stories had healed her mother merged with her shame and grief and, in trying to make sense of these fragmented thoughts, animals, once her mother's healers, became symbolic. Once this timeless travel was seen and witnessed, the young woman identified her moral injury and how trauma had turned her shame into a fear of the symbols of spirit healing that had once helped her mother. When the young woman was leaving that appointment, another client was waiting outside with her emotional therapy dog. The young woman approached the dog and asked if she could pet him. The other client said yes and the young woman kneeled at the dog, pet his head, and said, "Thank you. I am so, so sorry. You're a good dog". She returned to volunteering a week later and now owns a therapy dog that she takes with her to cheer up patients.

Trauma cannot be avoided or mitigated, nor can its impact be lessened through the training of the mind through resiliency programs. While resiliency programs may be helpful in learning coping skills for everyday adversity and crisis, their inability to identify trauma as moral injury can cause further spiritual crises. This, in turn, can lead to magnified feelings of displacement, alienation, despair, and suicidal thinking.

Once again, emotional trauma is a Moral Injury in need of soul repair. It is healed when this is recognized, integrated and addressed through the Pillars of the Spiritual, Cultural, Physical and Philosophical. To heal trauma, western behavioural psychology procedures need not only to be out of sight, but out of mind.

WALKABOUT

Non-verbal hurt, which is hurt experienced when one was non-verbal, is nevertheless stored in the cells of our body.

Our cells hold the memories of the event.

Experiences prior to mastering language are kept here.

Telling the story through a therapeutic sensory model will be more effective than through a narrative, as there were literally 'no words to express' or connect to the event(s).

SENSORY DIALOGUE

THE SENSE-ABLE STORY

When the Fear Guard responds to threat, it can interfere with the ability of the brain to encode and store certain information. This interference can make it difficult to remember the details of a traumatic experience, and difficult or impossible to recall traumatic events in their actual chronological order. Unfortunately, most modern counselling (as well as, in the legal context, victim and witness statements) employs methods based on what is referred to as ``chronological narratives". This is the 'who, what, where, when and why' style of inquiry which allegedly seeks to understand what exactly has happened to someone, and how it continues to affect them.

The way that information can be scrambled as a result of the fear response makes it unrealistic to expect people who have experienced trauma to recall and describe their traumatic experiences in a chronological narrative.

It is not surprising that a traumatized individual can feel that they are not being heard and understood when they are asked to describe, in a chronological narrative, what has happened to them. It is normal for there to be inconsistencies in the recalling and retelling of traumatic events. Furthermore, this kind of 'cognitive only' based questioning can evoke and re-traumatize the individual being assessed. In many circumstances, the more that the individual is asked to recall the incident (or incidents) through a cognitive narrative, the more disconnected and fearful the person might feel. This can fuel hypervigilance, resulting in more fear and which can often lead to a heightened mistrust of the world, both internally and externally.

Fortunately, there exists a better method than the conventional cognitive narrative approach to inquire about an incident. The body remembers reliably, through sensory memory. Sensory memory describes our ability to remember events through touch, smell, sight, sound, and taste. Trauma stories can be accessed by tapping into the sensory memory, where the trauma is stored. The body will continue to carry the story of the trauma in sensory memory until the trauma story is responsibly invoked and witnessed. In Tribal Theory this way of gathering information about the person's experience is referred to as 'Sensory Dialogue.'

When a client is guided towards and through recalling an event through sensory-based memory, they can more naturally, succinctly, and safely explain what they witnessed and, more importantly, how they felt at the time of the incident. Through this method, the person often feels less fearful, better heard, and witnessed. Sensory Dialogue can lead to a deeper sense of understanding and a heightened ability to make meaning of their traumatic response.

What does Sensory Dialogue look like in action?

Here are 3 scenario-based examples of Sensory Dialogue:

Example 1

Counsellor: I understand that you were inside the store when the store was being robbed. Do you remember any sounds or smells when you were in the store?

Client: I remember opening the cold storage fridge to reach for something and thinking the fridge wasn't cold enough for the food inside. And then a sound like a glass jar smashing on the ground. It must have been pickles or something with vinegar as I could smell it right after the sound. Just thinking about it is making me feel sick. I think I heard someone yelling. I can still smell the vinegar even talking to you right now and the robbery was two months ago.

Counsellor: That is okay. If that smell is still there, it is still there. You spoke about the fridge not being cold enough?

Client: Yeah, usually when you open the door on that fridge storage there is a gust of cold, I remember I didn't

134

feel that. Guess it wasn't working properly. It might have had something to do with the heat that day, it was midday and super hot out. I haven't been out much since that day. Just once with my daughter for coffee. Not because of the heat, well sort of, it reminds me of the shooting. Lately, when I feel the heat I begin to tremble and think about that day.

Counsellor: Is the smell of vinegar gone?

Client: Yes, but I remember now it was a jar, a big jar of pickled eggs that was sitting on the counter at the register. When I heard the smash, I turned and saw the person with a gun pointing to Jack.

Counsellor: Jack?

Client: Jack the owner of the store. I was so afraid. I froze. All I could smell was the vinegar. I froze. I saw Jack get shot. I froze!!! A hot sweltering day and I froze! I didn't stop him. I stood there and saw Jack get shot.

Counsellor: You know Jack is okay. He was shot in the arm, but he is okay.

Client: Yeah, I know. I am grateful he is ok. To be honest I am grateful I wasn't shot, I mean I was right there, he saw me, he didn't shoot me. He shot Jack and ran. Funny you know, my daughter and I were out for coffee together the other day and she ordered fries. She always smothers them in vinegar. She was asking me a question and I got so mad at her. I don't know why? I don't even remember what the question was. Now I am wondering if it was the smell of the vinegar. Could that make me lash out and yell for no reason. Could that smell remind me of how I froze and how I really wanted to yell? If so, no wonder I yelled. Guess I am still mad at myself for freezing.

In taking time to unpack the sensory with the person who was affected by an experience, the sensory story helps them 'make sense' of what they have been experiencing. This is how sensory dialogue leads to what Tribal Theory refers to as the 'sense-able story'. After engaging in sensory dialogue, and since the sensory story has been witnessed, the person is often then comfortable enough to start having insight on their trauma responses, moving aside the feelings of blame and shame that often accompany the inability to tell the cognitive narrative due to fragmented thought. This also leads to a person feeling more comfortable and safer in confiding further with the counsellor to integrate and make meaning of what has happened to them, not what is wrong with them.

Example 2

Counsellor: I understand that you are having a hard time sleeping since the incident?

Client: Yeah. It is not like I am awake worrying. I think I have dealt with a lot of the aftermath of the assault. I just wake up and can't get back to sleep.

Counsellor: Do you hear or smell anything that makes you wake up?

Client: No not really. In fact, I live above a bakery and those smells everyday make me feel cozy. If that makes sense?

Counsellor: That would definitely make me feel cozy and wanting a fresh cup of coffee and a croissant. What about hearing anything?

Client: I don't think so, my neighbourhood is pretty quiet.

Counsellor: Do you feel your body vibrate or sweat before you wake up completely?

Client: No. I do hear something that wakes me up though. The neighbours dog! He is a lovely dog but gets super excited when his owner comes home. They live two houses down and his owner takes him in the backyard when he gets home from work at 2 am. He is a bartender. Nice guy. Even knocked on doors in the neighbourhood to ask if his dog is disturbing anyone. Most of us know him and his dog so it was fine.

Counsellor: So, the dog and the owner have been there awhile, like before the assault.

Client: Oh yeah for a couple of years now. Funny the barking didn't use to wake me up, I got used to it pretty quickly.

Counsellor: Sounds like you knew the dog so didn't need to be alerted with his bark.

Client: Yep that is true. Hang on ... wait. I am shaking all of a sudden. I am thinking of the dog's bark and it is making me shake! I remember... the dog was barking; the dog was barking while I was being assaulted. I remember I wish I could yell but even if I do the dog's barking will cover it up. It is no use.

Counsellor: Does the dog bark only when his owner comes home?

Client: Yes! Oh my! The police asked me what time I thought I was attacked, and I couldn't answer them...the dog was barking! ... it must have been around 2 am!

Counsellor: I guess they might be able to confirm with your neighbour if he came home the night of the assault and what time?

Client: That is around the time I am waking up every night! I never thought it might be the dog. Maybe it is the sound of the dog that is now connected with the assault?

Counsellor: Maybe.

Client: No that would make sense! I think that is why I am waking up and not able to get back to sleep. I am waking up, as you would say, hypervigilant.

The interesting thing about this scenario was that the client would now be able to tell the police about the dog barking and possible time of the assault. It could then be confirmed by the neighbour. By asking about sensory, in this case sound, not only was the client able to make meaning of her waking at night, but it provided a timestamp for further police investigation. The client was able in the next session to change her lens on the dog barking as a fear association memory by befriending the dog. Her sleep improved and she herself adopted a rescue dog.

Example 3:

Client: I was thinking about sensory memories on my way here because we talked about them last week.

Counsellor: Great, any thoughts?

Client: Well one of my favourite things is this old blanket I had as a kid. I actually keep it in my closet, folded and placed inside my t-shirt pile. Kind of peeks out at me when I go into my closet everyday.

Counsellor: That sounds comforting.

Client: Maybe. I was thinking about why I liked it so much when I was a kid. It made me feel safe, I think. I would hide under it when my parents would fight, like a tent. I would pretend no one could find me and nothing could hurt me.

Counsellor: You said 'maybe'? Maybe it isn't comforting?

Client: Yeah, now I look at it and it makes me think not about feeling safe but brings back memories of all the fighting. It makes me feel sick at times. But I still let it stare at me. I am wondering if I should just throw it out. I know it sounds weird, but I am worried then I won't be safe.

Counsellor: What about just putting it out of sight? Just as a start to see if that helps.

Client: Yeah that would be a start. It kept me safe, almost like a friend. Like an invisible friend sort of.

This person ended up packing away the blanket in a spare backpack. In a few weeks he went on a spring hike with the backpack, blanket inside and went to a river where he used to go with his brother. His favourite place, he said. He took the blanket apart and left the wool pieces on the riverbank shore in the hope that the birds would gather it to make their nests. He said that he no longer feels nausea when he thinks of his parents fighting. He said he feels like the birds who nested in the blanket yarn have taken his fear into flight. He explained that he likes to think that because the blanket protected them, in return they have dispersed his fear into the wind when they fly.

This story is an example of the intertwining of Sensory Dialogue and Symbolics. Let's turn now to what Tribal Theory calls Symbolics and how it is helpful and essential in turning displacement and disorder into place, order, and a sense of belonging.

SYMBOLICS

Symbols which represent healing have been with us for ages. Many of these symbols evoke feelings of care, peace, and serenity. The Rod of Asclepius - the snake wrapped around the staff - for example, is a familiar symbol of the medical profession.

The creative approach of addressing and drawing meaning from our own stories through symbols has all but been abandoned by most Western counselling methods. Symbols which draw attention to contemporary causes (such as wearing a green ribbon to acknowledge mental health, or a pink shirt to bring attention to 'bullying') can be helpful for soliciting funds, but the importance of individual creative symbolism in trauma therapy has largely become ignored. Symbols can empower a person or a community's ability to tell the story of what has happened to them, and help them heal. Tribal Theory refers to working with symbols in counselling as Symbolics. The word combines 'symbol', a form of a sign that may have deep meaning, and 'ics', noting this as a field of study; the study of making meaning.

Through the combined use of Sensory Dialogue and Symbolics, the cognitive narrative style of therapy used in contemporary Western trauma counselling can be circumvented. We are provided with a fresh canvas on which a person can paint the profoundly healing sens-able stories, using their brush strokes to depict sensory feelings and symbols.

Here are 3 scenario-based examples of the application of Symbolics:

Example 1

Client: I have tons of anxiety all the time.

Counsellor: Often, Homebodies like yourself like to have things of comfort around; it's a way of nesting.

Client: Yes, this is true. You might think it silly, but ever since I was a kid, I've loved superheroes and I've collected superhero figurines all my life. I can't imagine not having them around me. Silly right?

Counsellor: I find that what people collect and hold on to has meaning to them. It even helps them to feel safe.

Client: My collection does make me feel good, but I've never thought of that as 'safe'.

Counsellor: Do you associate them with anything?

Client: I found my first figurine on the way home from school. It was sitting on top of a street drain cover and I didn't want it to fall in, so I picked it up. It was Batman figure. I remember thinking that someone must be sad to lose it, but I knew that there was no way to return it, so I kept it and went home.

Counsellor: It was like finding a treasure.

Client: Yes. I was so excited to show it to my dad when he got home, but he didn't come home that night. He didn't come home ever again.

Counsellor: That was the night of your dad's accident.

Client: Yes. I remember taking Batman out of my pocket and washing it then drying it with a paper towel and putting it beside my bed so I wouldn't forget to show my dad. He got home late most nights.

Counsellor: You said he was a firefighter.

Client: Yes. That was my first figurine, and it just grew from there. I have a couple hundred now. I remember holding that batman figure tight in my fist at my dad's funeral, thinking I hadn't shown it to my dad yet, I can't lose it. Everyone was talking about my dad being a hero, but all I could think about was that *my hero* was dead. I must have carried that batman everywhere for years after.

Counsellor: Do you still have it?

Client: Funny you should ask that. I actually took it out from my collector's cabinet today and placed it on my kitchen table while I had my morning coffee, just before I came here.

Counsellor: Symbolic things can have great meaning.

It was during the next session that this client said that he thought that all of these superheroes were symbols of his dad and that the more he had, the more he felt his dad's presence. Later, the client decided to host a celebration of life for his dad. He gathered his family and friends together, and gave them each a figurine. He still kept his collection, albeit a bit smaller, but felt he had honoured his dad by giving a bit of his dad's heroic energy to the people he cared for. He said that after doing this, for the first time, he visited his dad's grave, and buried the batman there. His dad would see it after all. The client was able to make meaning of his anxiety through this use of symbolics.

Example 2

In this example, a Crisis Worker is with a woman in her 30's who was just in a car accident with her grandmother. Her grandmother is in critical condition in the emergency ward.

Granddaughter: Do you think my Gran will be okay? That other car just came out of nowhere through a red light.

Crisis Worker: Everyone is doing their best. The police are investigating the accident. Is that your Gran's purse?

Granddaughter: Yeah it is. It was her sisters. Gran says she carries it so that her sister is always with her.

Crisis Worker: That is sweet. Is there anyone I can call? Your father or mother?

Granddaughter: No. My parents died when I was three years old in a boating accident and my Gran raised me.

Time passes, and the doctor comes out to speak with the granddaughter and tell her that her grandmother did not survive. The crisis worker stays with the woman for an hour or so before leaving when the woman's husband arrives. As the crisis worker leaves, the granddaughter gently takes her arm.

Granddaughter: I guess it is my turn to carry this purse for both my Gran and her sister.

Crisis Worker: I think that is a lovely thought, sweet just like your Gran.

To be aware of and to acknowledge symbolic items can help people connect and create meaning even in the midst of a crisis or tragedy. Symbolic items can present themselves when we look for them. For crisis workers, the Symbolic Story is often more important than the narrative of what happened. It can be an important anchor of meaning to help a person weathering a storm.

Example 3

Client: It is so difficult for me to go to court mediation and face my ex-partner. I don't know why; you know my job. I am so strong and confident in that, but I can't seem to draw on that strength at all when I am in the same room as him. I turn into a weakling.

Counsellor: Does it help to tell yourself 'I can do this' before the mediation appointment?

Client: I have tried that on many occasions and it just doesn't work. It actually makes it worse.

Counsellor: What activities do you like that have a strong sensory component for you? A feel or smell that you like while you do them?

Client: I would say baking for the smell and the warmth of the kitchen. Knitting for the feel of the wool and the sound of the needles clicking.

Counsellor: Could either of those activities come into the mediation appointment with you? A symbol you can carry for strength?

Client: I picked up my knitting the other day and it helped me distract my anxious thoughts. Maybe I could knit a scarf and wear it for strength.

Counsellor: There is an idea. What if as you knit you think about your strengths and everything you have overcome? Like a prayer blanket that people make for cancer survivors, except this is your strength scarf.

Client: It's worth a try. I am going to pick up wool on the way home. Lots of orange and red, my favourite colors, in a cozy baby wool.

This client knit a strength scarf and wore it to her next court mediation session with her ex-partner. The counsellor received a call a few days after the mediation.

"I put on the scarf and walked right in, feeling strong and confident", said the client, "it was amazing".

In crisis, adversity and trauma, the universality of Symbolics and Sensory Dialogue hold the power to make meaning. Using colours, textures, nature, animals, and our gifts of creativity, we can create our own spiritual healing.

NOTES

FOR THE LOVE OF A 'SILL-Y' CAT
ILLUSTRATION AND CONSIDERATION

I didn't know what to do. The fire had consumed the whole house. People were so generous giving me things, and the other tenants too. I was lucky to be alive, I kept telling myself, over and over again. But I couldn't stop shaking and it didn't help that every time I breathed in through my nose I could still smell 'burnt'. I decided to meet with someone, who had been offered by victim services in our community. I figured maybe they could tell me something that would help these pictures in my head turning over and over again, especially of the cat. My cat had been carried out by my neighbour, since I was carried out on a gurney. I had broken my leg two weeks earlier. The cat I couldn't get out of my head was the alley cat that used to sit on my window sill, only when the window was closed. I had fed him for about three months and the way he would look at me through the window, his eyes open wide, almost like he was smiling through them. I had named him 'Silly', lame I know, but I felt like my window 'sil' was his home. My own cat totally ignored him. She showed no interest or jealousy when I would feed him. I like to think she knew he just needed someone and that someone was us. Since the fire, I could not get the picture of Silly's eyes out of my mind. They were imprinted on the back of my eyelids. I was worried about where he was, who would feed him, and worse, that he might have died. I was hesitant to go see

149

someone. Talking about my feelings was not something I usually did, and to be honest, I didn't know how I felt, just not right. So, I went. I was introduced to someone who called themselves a crisis and trauma counsellor. I thought, okay, trauma really? I remember the counsellor asking me about the fire by remembering through sounds, smells and touch, quite odd I thought, but I was amazed how much I was able to tell them, as I had tried to remember things since the fire but was unsuccessful. Frozen, was the way it was described by the counsellor, and that is the way it felt. I was also asked about things I like to do, how I like to spend my time, and about what had been happening to me since the fire. This counsellor explained the role of a Hunter and the role of a Homebody and I quickly identified with the Homebody. When I was asked about animals I connect with, I started to cry. Sob, actually. And then I talked about 'Silly'. It wasn't long until it hit me...the impact of worrying about Silly. I didn't know where he was, so in a sense, 'my sense' everyone was not safe, someone was still missing. I realized within moments that as a Homebody, this would be devastating to me, and until I found out what happened, I would not rest. There was no guarantee I would ever find Silly and the counsellor asked me what I might consider doing to honour Silly and our time together. I answered without hesitation, help other cats. And that is what I did. As soon as I applied to work for a cat shelter, the eyes of Silly no longer haunted me. I work there permanently now, after two years of volunteering. Every time a cat comes in, I thank Silly for sending them to me.

I know, it is obvious I didn't find Silly. My hope is that he has found another window sill, but if not, if he did die, I envision him in cat heaven, building a treehouse with a window and sill to sit on. I know now, that by doing what my Authentic Homebody would do and listening to the guidance of my Healthy Guard I was able to move forward with a purpose and make some meaning of what happened.

31 year old former assistant daycare teacher now an animal rescuer

NOTES

TribaLORE: Janis

From a very young age, the Hunter inside of Janis knew that she had to get away from her family of origin. Born into a poor working-class family, surrounded by the violence of an alcoholic stepfather, there were very few expectations of Janis as a child. Yet, she always found her way as a hunter, long before she had identified as one through the Tribal Theory framework.

"At one point, I was forced to stay home after school to look after my little sister, and I became so bossy and miserable. Finally, my mum hired a sitter, and I went and got a job and started contributing to the household. It was a grounding experience; I was back on my path as a Hunter."

After floundering in her early twenties, struggling with an eating disorder and leaving a relationship with an abusive, controlling man, Janis understood that she had to do something. She identified her desire to feel control and that she wanted and needed to find enough control in her life to feel safe. At twenty-eight, Janis became the first person in her family to attend University.

Enrolled in University, Janis became an Ontario scholar in her first term and remained one until she graduated with an MA in sociology. Now a self-identified feminist psychotherapist, Janis believes in equalizing power structures through encouraging self-disclosure, unconditional acceptance, and never talking down to people.

"I always tell the women who come to me: I don't care what you did to get here - I'm just so happy that you're here." she says, describing her practice.

Living and practicing in North Western Ontario for twenty years, Janis worked from an indigenous model; a model which understands that the racism in that region and others is the end product of 500 years of oppression and cultural genocide. Janis worked on the vanguard of EMDR (Eye movement desensitization and reprocessing), becoming one of the most acknowledged therapists in that field. She married a man she describes as her perfect partner - a homebody. She became a registered psychotherapist five years ago after years of counselling and advocating for people through women's centres and sexual assault centres, tirelessly fighting for justice.

It hasn't always been easy for Janis to uncover her path. In order to become certified as a registered psychotherapist, despite years of already working in the field, Janis had to work in mainstream, 'male-stream' institutions, environments drastically different from what she was accustomed to. In one of these agencies, she worked with a manager who constantly micro-managed her.

"It was bad for a Hunter like me. I was a Hunter being hunted and I was in constant flight mode. I just wanted to work." she says of that experience. Despite these adverse environments, Janis received her certification.

Certified, Janis began working for an agency in Thunder Bay and found results in the work she did there. However, the conventional workplace structure of that environment was still not the right fit for her. With the encouragement of the other women working in her field, Janis developed a private practice and began looking for models of psychotherapy that identify how the body and spirit connect. Searching the internet, she discovered Tribal Theory. Struck by the model's accessible language, comprehensive application, and it's unique adaptability, Janis immediately identified Tribal Theory's capacity to speak to both the head and the heart.

"This model unites the thinking brain and the feeling body." It creates new neural pathways, and calms down the body.' Janis describes the strengths of working with the Tribal Theory model, "It divides people into two categories: the hunters, who are quick and logical, and the homebodies, who are emotional. The language around 'gifts' is empowering, and allows people to see what they have formerly understood as weaknesses as their assets. The model is not only non-colonial, unlike conventional western methods, but actively *decolonial*. It addresses cellular trauma carried in DNA. It's a whole new radical paradigm; it works quicker, sees results faster, especially in the Indigenous Peoples communities. It heals intergenerational trauma. And the word is out!"

Since adopting the model, Janis has brought Barbara Allyn to Thunder Bay to train more therapists. Individuals from northern communities are flown to Thunder Bay to work with Janis and her colleagues. The Tribal Theory model is seeing widespread results in that region. On a personal level, Tribal Theory has empowered Janis to understand her own gifts, and to be excited about them. It has enhanced her ability to share knowledge, and to build concepts as a psychotherapist.

INTERGENERATIONAL TRAUMA
ECHOES OF THE ELDERS

"Our Ancestors knew that healing comes in
cycles and circles"
Gemma B. Benton

Tribal Theory operates on the idea that our body remembers. We now know that memories are stored in cells all over our body and that our cellular memories, influenced by our environment, carry that influence to subsequent generations. Regarding trauma, this is known as intergenerational trauma.

Tribal Theory uses the retelling of your story to shift intergenerational moral injury by telling your cells a different story (a story of survival). Trauma carried by cells from a prior generation or generations is given new meaning and, with this meaning, trauma shifts and is reattached to cells as historical tales, not terrors. In the retelling of the story, the Fear Guard steps down and the Healthy Guard steps in.

The Authentic Self is acknowledged as are the authentic selves of those who experienced the trauma carried via DNA. The cellular memory carries trauma from generation to generation, waiting until that trauma story is revealed and retold by the Healthy Guard. The changing of the guard takes place as soon as we can make meaning.

This is why the Healthy Guard Guide and Fear Guard Protector above the Trauma Life Line is so important. When retelling the story, understood first through the Fear Guard Protector then through the Healthy Guard, you are retelling the story to every cell in your body that presented in Fear Guard (to your cellular memories).

Tribal Theory responds to the echoes of the Elders, past and present, who come forward carrying their healing traditions and wisdom, asking those who feel helpless and hopeless to acknowledge their authentic role, their genius, their healer.

By exploring the ways to connect with their authentic selves, a Hunter or Homebody can access the healing ways and medicine of the traditional Healthy Guard, to support and heal themselves and others. Intergenerational Moral Injury, cellular trauma held, waiting to be witnessed, requires both sensory and symbolic to acknowledge the soul's story and bring the soul injury into the present.

157

Intergenerational Moral Injury can only be healed through the application of the cultural, spiritual, and customary ways of those who carry the wounds.

How families, groups, nations and people have walked in the world, their way of 'being' needs to be respected, accepted, maintained and cherished.

In doing so, there is purpose. In 'being' so, there is meaning.

TribaLORE: Marilyn writes her story

My name is Marilyn Lewis, I was the sixth child in a family of eight. I come from a family where I felt I belonged and loved despite the chaos I grew up in. Both my parents were residential school survivors where they learned a lot of unhealthy behaviors. These were passed down to our generation where I am probably the only one in our family who has attempted to heal from this legacy. I had one male child who is now an adult. He has blessed me with four grandchildren and extended to nine great grandchildren. The youngest of my grandchildren who is in his early twenties is the only one who is starting to break the cycle of having children in the teen years. I'm also the only one in my family who has completed graduate studies. This is all due to my late mother who believed in me that I can succeed. Unfortunately, none of my siblings completed high school.

In hindsight, the biggest challenge for me has been not honoring my authentic role as a "Homebody". I have always been propelled into roles that were not a fit. This is due to my advanced education getting promoted to management positions when my passion was always a frontline worker as a therapist. This is the role where I feel most authentic. I felt like I was always meeting society's expectations of moving upwards rather than staying in a role I was comfortable with.

With my education and work with my own people, Indigenous people, I became aware of the depth of trauma we have suffered as a result of colonization. I was always in search of a model that would fit working with intergenerational trauma. Of course, when I came across a flyer on "Tribal Theory" I had to explore it. The term "Tribal" and "decolonizing approach to trauma" caught my attention.

When I started to learn about Tribal Theory, it was an "aha moment" for me. I felt validated that there was a reason why I didn't feel comfortable in my position as a Clinical Supervisor, that it is 'OK" to be you and not conform to society's expectations. I will eventually go back to my original passion in private practice part time once I finish my contracts. There were times in my 30+ career where I held my authentic position and those were the most fulfilling jobs I've held.

In my role as a Clinical Supervisor I am able to share about tribal theory and understand why people are not happy in their roles and their place in them. I can identify a homebody and a hunter with the people I supervise and encourage them to pursue roles where they would thrive. Too often, people are placed in roles that are not a fit and they themselves are not aware why they are unhappy in their positions.

Tribal Theory framework has helped me to identify and be aware when in a "displaced position" to preserve my authentic self while doing so.

For anyone with a difficult life story, it is my hope that they learn that it is "Ok" to follow your passion, and not get influenced by society's expectations. I find you are most at peace being your authentic self. It is a long journey without proper guidance. Tribal Theory resonates with my authentic self.

TRIBAL THEORY

A GLOBAL CANVAS FOR THE ART OF HEALING PRACTICES

"these mountains that you are carrying, you were only supposed to climb"

Najwa Zebian

Tribal Theory works as a foundation upon which many global healing practices can be supported. While exploring this framework you will discover how by first acknowledging the authentic self, we are better able in discovering which practices work best for the Hunter and which are best suited for the Homebody.

Observe how the cognitive response in the Hunter, one with a natural energy to spend, takes a straight forward path in processing information. Recognize the Homebody, adept at conserving energy, takes a path that is longer and more complex in nature. Considering these differences when beginning to apply therapeutic methodology and healing practices supports their respective journeys to their authentic well being.

For example: Tribal Theory has found that the practice of EMDR, which utilizes eye movements as a form of bilateral stimulation, works better for Hunters who are carrying trauma. Brain Spotting, which focuses the eye on a fixed gaze position, is best suited for Homebodies carrying trauma. Sitting meditation finds excellent application in Homebodies, but Hunters often prefer a moving meditation that uses rhythm to focus and center the mind. Narratives while walking can be helpful for Hunters, whereas journaling works well for Homebodies. Even studies in animal therapy have shown that Hunter characteristics seem to connect more with dogs while Homebodies characteristics tend to connect with cats (although many of us seem to have a domestic menagerie to make sure we are safely covered!).

Focusing on the best-suited methodology for each individual - nurturing their nature - can make a tremendous difference in meeting the needs of their authentic self. Importantly, feelings of failure, frustration, or even shame in not being able to connect or follow through with certain therapeutic models can be avoided. Beginning by simply considering the authentic role of each person creates better outcomes for those in pain and their healers.

THE TRIBE OF FIRST RESPONDERS

FIRST RESPONDERS

I have had the honour of working with first responders for most of my career. When I first began to work with Tribal Theory, first responders were a foundational 'tribe' with whom I could apply this new framework.

This next chapter has been drawn from my experience working with first responders and will give you a sense of how I have interpreted the prominent Tribal roles of firefighter, police officer, and paramedic through Tribal Theory. Tribal Theory has been invaluable in assisting me while working with first responders as they take on the emotional toll that accompanies caring for and protecting our communities. Tribal Theory empowers them to identify moral injury, see the genius of anxiety, and, when needed, move toward post-traumatic growth.

THE FIREFIGHTER

"I became a firefighter because I wanted to save people. But I should have been more specific. I should have named names." - Firefighter

The Firefighter is an authentic Homebody. They go into a blaze to save the heart of the home. Their connection and understanding of how to keep a safe place for people to land is at the core of everything they do, including safety in their own environment. If you have ever travelled from one firehouse to another, you will see that each one has its own sense of home. The firefighter protects the hearth. They are storytellers. Their dinner table is where the family lands. They are there to help the community breathe and they are interwoven with the community in a quiet, participatory way. They keep track of everything and everyone. Firefighters do not fight people; they fight an element that can hurt arbitrarily. This is the role of the Homebody - to keep the fire in control and to keep it a useful element.

The firefighter is the warmth provider. A firefighter's most difficult situation is not the fire itself, but when they see the body of someone in the remains of the fire, especially if this person is close in age to someone close to them. Firefighters are big-ticket item buyers. This is how they often, maladaptively, move through their trauma response. They are extremely aware that a safe place to land can disappear at any time and that a natural element is what can take it away. A traumatized firefighter who has not made meaning of their experiences can take on a 'live for today' attitude because there is no guarantee of tomorrow.

A firefighter who is responding to trauma will also try to control their private home base and the individuals therein. An otherwise open, sharing, family gatherer will present as firm, controlling, and even abusive to others in their own home, while still maintaining their Homebody caring presentation outside the home. The firefighter often couples with a person who is emotionally distant. It is their way of trying to care for someone in need. It can be exhausting on a personal level because a firefighter needs to connect with someone who can empathize intuitively and help them recharge and see that they don't get too tough on themselves when losses of life happen.

Heart issues will show up in firefighters more than any other illness. Some illness is, of course, due to environmental pollution caused by smoke or a collapse, but other forms of damage are present in the firefighters who have tried to fight a fire and feel like they failed to create a safe place for others. If they feel they were not able to carry out their duty, a spiritual discourse will result often manifesting as heart problems and cardiovascular disease. Since the Homebody response to fear is to freeze and turn inward, they may develop strange aversions to foods; eating disorders; self-harm behaviors in the form of cutting, bone-breaking or suicide attempts by overdose, single car accidents or car fumes. They will find ways to cut the oxygen off because they have failed to give oxygen, (life) to someone else.

THE POLICE OFFICER

"Every time, when I go to a domestic call where there is a young kid, I remember. I make sure I find a way to smile at them." - Police Officer

A police officer can be either a Homebody or a Hunter who spends a lot of time in the position of guard. If, before becoming a police officer, the person has been able to be their authentic selves and have honed their healthy guard, they are great candidates for this work.

As a Hunter, they will bring a sense of scope and awareness of everything around them. In healthy guard they can detect noises in the background, shadows in the dark, and the scent of danger. This makes them a natural fit for street policing, field investigating, and training others.

The Homebody police officer, with a Healthy Guard, is intuitive about others, can step back and take in a situation, and can de-escalate others by giving them space and listening well. They are wonderful at community policing, as they carry an innate determination to create a safe place.

Taking on the duties of a police officer as a Hunter or Homebody possessing a Healthy Guard creates a person who does their job with instinct and compassion because they have built the required resilience.

Challenges arise when a Hunter or Homebody has lived most of their life in Fear guard. In doing so, they have not been able to discover their authentic self or build much resilience. They are more vulnerable to responding negatively to others in both the broader community and their own work community. People who live in fear guard most of their lives will often believe that this is the only place they fit or belong. Guard is the only position they know, so they choose to police, not aware that they are bringing an unhealthy guard with them and coming from a fear guard position with all of its negative consequences.

Healthy Guards are a unique group. These members of the Tribe are made up of some of the healthiest Hunters and Homebodies. They have the ability to recognize the Fear Guard in others. Just by being in the role of Healthy Guard, they help to show others how to guard without fear. These guards create and take pride in the community, and do what they can to keep others as saf as possible.

They are welcomed mediators and detectors o other's needs, concerns, and fears. They are not there t be the law but to uphold the laws of human nature interacting when required, creating a space for negotiatio when necessary, and working toward peaceful resolutions

Police who have joined the policing community from Fear Guard position will struggle with those presenting i Fear Guard. They will respond to those in the Fear Guard as though they are looking into a mirror. Coming face t face with their own fears they use negative energy and force in their day-to-day interactions with the public.

This is the root of 'good cop, bad cop'. The mixture of healthy guards and fear guards creates a polarization ir the police forces where the healthy guards try to help the community to flourish safely while the fear guards become fearfully guarded. With little experience or no experience in being a healthy guard, the fear guard finds it difficult to carry on his duty without exploding (displaced Hunter) or imploding (displaced Homebody).

People who have lived in Fear Guard most of their lives must find ways to make meaning and integrate what has happened to them and move into the Healthy Guard Guide before taking on an official position of a guard in our tribe.

THE PARAMEDIC

"My role as a paramedic isn't always to save a life. Sometimes it is to simply make their transition comfortable."

Australian Paramedic

Paramedics are authentic Hunters. Paramedics hunt for the challenges of the holistic self in both the organic and the transitional world. They are the first responders and the witness to the human and cellular energy transition between life and death. They work with this cellular energy to carry out the wishes of their 'patient'. They are the angels with their wings tucked in.

Like a Hunter, the paramedic needs to do a consistent walk-a-about to be able to process the enormity of their role. Without them, the rest of the tribe would have no holistic nourishment and, although the police (new Guard) is the protector from a wild or man-made invasion of the tribe, the paramedic (Hunter) holds the sustenance of life; it hunts to feed the body, mind and soul.

Sadly, these first responders are often overlooked.

Although they are the first to take a 'hands on' approach to the needs of people they also, as stated before, are witness to the cellular whole body trauma response to an event where 'the question of life' lies. They selflessly align their intuitive being with the patient in need. Their cellular energy merges with the patient, connecting in the most healing way. They act as a guide, and this role requires consistent nurturing and rejuvenation through nature.

Hunters are organically intertwined with nature. They get their strength from the living natural world and, without a connection to nature, they begin to question their work and wonder why their work goes unseen by so many of the tribe. The tribe needs to acknowledge the work of the paramedic. It is the most challenging of positions in our modern responders as the paramedic will accumulate the cellular trauma of their patients. Without recognition from the tribe of the toll this can take on them, a paramedic may experience a true dis-connect from others.

The Hunter will feel that they are being 'hunted'-actually 'haunted' by the images they have experienced in their work. These hauntings embedded in Moral Injury can lead Paramedics, so connected to the spiritual, to question their purpose on earth and take their own lives, death by despair. They often find natural settings and natural material to do so.

Paramedics are, in essence, 'spiritual witnesses' who are often asked by their patients to act as 'spiritual advisors'. They are not like the Homebody Medicine Person who accesses the cellular body to nurture it towards a healthy holistic well-being. They are the Spiritual connection to 'All That Is'. They witness the transition from the human body to energy and the decision of the patient to move on or stay. They are witness to the true 'science' of nature. A paramedic would not transfer into the role of a doctor very well unless it was work in Emergency response medicine. The confined 'science' of medicine and its current disconnect with the cellular energy of the spirit can be a frustration for a paramedic.

Paramedics are the hand holders and witnesses, the comfort and connection for other humans going through trauma. They respond to patients who are on a continuum of being consumed by fear or full of acceptance to their fate.

Paramedics witness, experience and honour the decisive moments of science, philosophy and spirituality combined. The three circles of life as we know it.

A FIRST RESPONDER AND TRIBAL SPEAK

There are endless benefits both personally and professionally to understanding tribal theory, even at its most basic level. Because of tribal theory I have a better understanding of who I am and how I fit into this world as an individual, a family member, a friend, a co-worker. Personally, tribal theory has redefined my past and provided a different perspective for the future.

My past–wrought with personal crisis and professional confliction- is reframed with the understanding of my genuine place within my tribe. Self blame, doubt and low self esteem is replaced with true understanding, contentment and self awareness. The puzzle pieces of life seem to fit better and for longer. My future choices are made with the education and awareness of my valued place and as naturally as the seasons change, happiness always finds me –my true self. So many of us are forced into roles/jobs/careers due to outside pressures, expectations and commitments. The majority are not happy and can never figure out why. The simple answer, based on tribal theory, is that we are outside of our natural roles. We are trying to fit a round block into a square hole.

Working in the police industry, I am now instinctively aware of those colleagues who are in their defined role as a hunter or a guard and those who are forcing the round block into the square hole. It does not come as a surprise that those who are forcing the pieces are also in regular conflict with their peers and supervisors.

As a victim services worker, I am able to have an insight into my clients genuine place within the tribe. I am able to better craft coping skills and methods based on this —even if they are unaware of tribal theory. I am able to help them succeed and move past trauma utilizing tribal theory insights.

Additional Applications for Tribal Theory

Teaching notes courtesy of
Michaela Bottle

FAMILY MATTERS

"I have three kids; two are Homebodies and one is a Hunter. I am a dog person and I began seeing that it is like having two yellow Labs and a Jack Russell, and instantly was able to change my parenting for the better."

Parent and Emergency Nurse

CLASS 'WITH LOTS OF' ROOM
TO BE YOUR AUTHENTIC SELF

"My classroom is now a place of learning, with students focused on their studies while striving towards emotional well-being for each other and themselves...Tribal Theory is a simple miracle!"

Grade 7 Teacher

Tribal Theory has a simple application in the classroom. A teacher can use Tribal Theory to help students identify their authentic roles and then teach *to* those roles. In making the classroom a tribal community, each student is accepted for the authentic role that they have in the class and this creates meaning, safety and, in turn, coping skills. The classroom becomes a place of support and acceptance - a safe place to land, where there are no misfits, only members of the Tribe.

COMMUNITY DISASTER
MITIGATING TRAUMA IN THE TRIBE

"When I was a boy and I would see scary things in the news, my mother would say to me, "Look for the helpers. You will always find people who are helping."

Fred Rogers

THE FLOOD

A flood has happened in a rural area. The emergency management team consists of a team lead and three others who need to inform and organize a school gym of 600 people who have fled to this designated evacuation centre.

When the emergency team lead scans the people in front of her within a Tribal Theory framework, she can quickly identify the Homebodies, and Hunters, as well as who is in Healthy Guard and who is in Fear Guard.

The Homebodies are naturally putting up cots, giving out blankets, checking or creating nutritional needs, or 'being in the moment' physically holding others or lending an ear. The Healthy Guards, the resilient Homebodies or Hunters, are walking the perimeter, and keeping an eye out for the Fear Guards that may need extra attention or may be de-escalating, as the Fear Guards can react with anger both emotionally and/or physically.

The Hunters, if they have not already, are grabbing any vehicle that will move and they are off to Hunt for more survivors, food, or other needed supplies.

Within the Tribal Theory framework, understanding the mirror neuron imaging of our brains, which helps us identify people who are 'like' us, becomes a very useful tool.

The Authentic Homebody in the team is designated to lead the Homebody community, the Authentic Hunter to go out and support the Hunters, and the most experienced, resilient team and team leader to hang with the Healthy Guards and also observe the people in Fear Guard.

The innate connection of a Homebody to another Homebody creates a core understanding of the authentic role and how that authentic role can naturally respond to the needs of others. This connection creates a sense of purpose in doing for others, and makes meaning of their responses while still involved in the event. By doing so, this means the brain, at first in a fragmented response, can start to make meaning and this creates a mind, body understanding of purpose. The neurons in both the brain and the gut are given a job, a purpose and the response goes from fragmentation to connection. It's a connection with the authentic self to do what it is meant to do and a connection with others; a sense of helping others survive. In each, the authentic self-response is also sensory. By connecting Homebodies with Homebodies and Hunters with Hunters sensory needs are intuitively met and the memories connected to the sensory can again attach to purpose and meaning.

The Healthy Guard (a Hunter or Homebody who chooses to take on a guarded position because of the strong, healthy coping strategies and integration through their own lives) is capable of 'intuiting' and 'feeling' the people in and going out of the gym. They are able to detect those who are responding in Fear Guard and often able to intuit which authentic role the Fear Guarded person has been displaced from.

They can then give the displaced person an authentic role activity that can be extremely helpful and de-escalate an individual or group of individuals.

In responding to an event where a community has been affected, Tribal Theory gives people purpose and meaning has the ability to mitigate trauma 'in the moment' by 'meeting people where they are at.'

"Instead of praising people for being resilient, change the systems that are making them vulnerable."

Dr. Muna Abdi

AUTHOR'S NOTE

Contemporary Western psychology often fails to address, or even completely ignores, the spiritual component of moral injury. This is currently evidenced by lack of attention given to 'spiritual beliefs' in the training of psychologists and counsellors. This effectively discredits the traditions of other cultural approaches, and even goes so far as to invoke negative associations with those who practice outside of the Western lens. This has, in turn, perpetuated exclusively Western ideas of mental health. What constitutes normal or abnormal is purposefully and strategically defined by the distorted biases of unreal cultural supremacy. By ignoring the human spirit and a plethora of global traditional perspectives, the beliefs of others that don't adhere to the Western lens of mental health are being eradicated.

Underlying all of this is the message that one possesses no spirit, that one has no authentic purpose, and that one is only understood through one's 'maladapted' behaviours. In the framework of Tribal Theory, the *spiritual* is addressed *first*.

ABOUT THE AUTHOR

Barbara Allyn

Trauma Therapist/Advanced Crisis Intervenor

ACTT, ACI (she/her)

Barbara Allyn is a thought leader, trauma response professional and the creator of Tribal Theory. She is a certified trauma therapist and crisis-intervention counsellor with 35-years' experience in active, front-line crisis response. Barbara has evolved into a paradigm shifter through her ground-breaking work on Sensory Dialogue, Symbolics & Moral Injury.

Barbara is a highly respected speaker, presenter and facilitator, who brings a wealth of experiential learning from her work as a crisis intervenor, family mediator and education behavioural specialist. Her development of the Tribal Theory framework is consistently described by frontline responders, mental health professionals and communities as practical and easy-to-apply, by creating a powerful long-term path to integration, healing, and well-being.

Tribal Theory is a global framework that has been met with enthusiasm and applause and integrated into trauma-informed practices worldwide.

Barbara is available for virtual & in person conferences and workshops internationally.

For information on booking speaking events or workshops (both in person or virtual)

contact@tribaltheoryglobal.com

TribaLORE arts + science

Ontario, Canada

www.tribaltheoryglobal.com

Made in the USA
Monee, IL
13 February 2021

60431113R00115